The Best of AMERICAN DREAM HOMES

THE NATION'S PREMIER HOME MAGAZINE

Published in the United States of America
in 2007 by Hanley Wood, LLC

Hanley Wood, LLC
One Thomas Circle, NW, Suite 600
Washington, DC 20005

Vice President, Home Plans, Andrew Schultz
Associate Publisher, Development, Jennifer Pearce

Director, Marketing, Mark Wilkin
Editor, Simon Hyoun
Assistant Editor, Kimberly R. Johnson
Publications Manager, Brian Haefs
Production Manager, Theresa Emerson
Graphic Artist, Joong Min
Product Manager, Susan Jasmin
Marketing Manager, Brett Bryant

Most Hanley Wood titles are available at quantity discounts
with bulk purchases for educational, business, or sales promotional
use. For information, please contact Andrew Schultz
at aschultz@hanleywood.com.

VC Graphics, Inc.
President/Creative Director, Veronica Claro Vannoy
Senior Designer, Denise Reiffenstein
Senior Designer, Jennifer Gerstein
Designer, Jeanne-Erin Worster

Front Cover Photograph © Dan Forer / Forer Incorporated
Back Cover Photograph © John Sciarrino

Distribution Center
PBD
Hanley Wood Consumer Group
3280 Summit Ridge Parkway
Duluth, Georgia 30096

10 9 8 7 6 5 4 3 2 1

Library of Congress Control Number 2006935013

ISBN-13 978-1-931131-72-8
ISBN-10 1-931131-72-4

Printed and bound in China

The Best of AMERICAN
DREAM HOMES
THE NATION'S PREMIER HOME MAGAZINE

Edited by Lisa S. Siglag and Simon Hyoun

CONTENTS

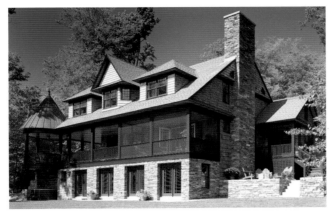

Introduction

Since its premier issue in 2002, *American Dream Homes* magazine has featured the best residential accomplishments of architects, designers, and builders from across the nation. Each issue told the accounts of determined owners who realized their visions of the ideal home. After publishing hundreds of such stories, from the simplest vacation renovation to the most ambitious new construction, the magazine as a whole began to tell the tale of the ingenious individuality of every dream home. It was as if every great idea of a home, longing to be built, always broke somewhat from established historical styles, even as it invoked them.

Sometimes the break was necessary to the home's location—as in the case of this book's first home, a Shingle-style coastal home built unusually high to peer over the tops of sand dunes. At other times, a home turned against tradition for beauty and function—as in the book's final home, a straight-and-narrow Shed with playful spaces and gently civilized rustic details. Certainly there were larger, affluent homes—the crowd-pleasing Hampton estate with glorious formalities (page 68). But over and over it was clear that a dream home, even when familiar in description, could always prove an exciting encounter.

The other trend that emerged from the magazine's stories was how modern methods and building technologies enabled and elevated—rather than compromised—historical designs. Against purism, the reality of the American dream home was that it had be a home of today. Layouts anticipated and responded to the everyday use of resident families and invited guests. Spaces were comfortably luxurious and amenitized to the hilt. The construction of the home looked to be environmentally responsible and socially conscious. For instance, the National Association of Home Builders took extraordinary care to incorporate sustainable and alternative materials and fuel-saving products into their ENERGY STAR®-rated concept home (page 102). By selecting technology that could be built in and work unseen, the home made fewer compromises in style for function. The result was a thoroughly progressive home with a regionally appropriate Spanish-American exterior and resort-style way of living.

This is the first-ever collection of the very best from the past four years of *American Dream Homes*. These 30 homes represent all the recent advances and trends in the custom home industry—not to mention tremendous positive responses from the magazine's loyal readers. Let your armchair tour of these real-life homes inform and inspire visions of your own dream home.

Lisa S. Siglag
Simon Hyoun

TRADITIONAL ELEGANCE

*W*e learn and draw from our past. In literature, books are made into plays and movies; in art, contemporary painters gain inspiration from the old masters; and in architecture and design, traditional forms are cherished and re-created.

Why do traditional homes have such a broad appeal? Perhaps it's the fine craftsmanship and details—such as the Palladian windows of a Colonial house, the welcoming porches of a plantation home, or the turrets on a Victorian—that remind us of the homes that raised and comforted us.

In this section, seven new houses call to mind designs that flourished centuries ago. Some of the residences include precise replicas of traditional elements, while others are more loosely based on classic structures. And though all of the homes afford an old-time flavor, the amenities offer modern-day appeal. For example, in a New Jersey Shingle-style home, a genre that dates from the 1880s, traditional elements like bead-board walls and coffered ceilings give structure to 21st-Century visions of life at home. These traditional homes contain all the charm of those days gone by, without denying modern conveniences.

Crisp white railings and mouldings bring a dramatic counterpoint to unfinished shingles.

Creating a *Classic*

Dating from the 1880s, Shingle-style houses were generally built in summer-vacation destinations due to their easy-going appearance. Houses built prior to this style had a much more fussy quality. For example, Victorian houses featured an abundance of Queen Anne spindlework and Italianate detailing, whereas Shingle-style homes were devoid of such ornamentation. Today, examples of the classic style—wooden shingles, peaked irregular rooflines, and plenty of windows and porches—can be found in the Northeast, such as on Cape Cod, the Jersey shore, and in the Hamptons.

The ocean-front Mantoloking, New Jersey house shown here includes many features characteristic of the late-19th-Century style. Beautifully created by architect John Lederer of Lederer & Wright Partnership in Bay Head, New Jersey, the house required one year to plan and two years to build. Lederer took that time to work closely with the owners, who yearned not only for a house rich with traditional features that would let the home appear as if it had been there for 100 years, but for a place where their whole family could gather comfortably. With both goals in mind, Lederer designed steeply-pitched varied rooflines to give architectural interest to the exterior, and covered and screened porches to greet visitors with a gracious and intimate welcome. At the back of the home, a dramatic multistory tower outfitted with mullioned bay windows conveys classic style. Small windows placed on a diagonal emphasize the tower's height. On all sides of the house, crisp white railings and trim provide a nice counterpoint to the heavier, organic shingles.

Incorporating a tower into the architecture is
appropriate to the home's late-19th-Century style.

The traditional yet welcoming atmosphere continues inside. Interior designer Vicki McLoughlin came out of retirement to help the homeowners work on the seven-bedroom house. To take advantage of the waterfront views, the main rooms were placed on the upper level. And although the homeowners took a traditional approach to the design of the home, they did make one unconventional decision—to eliminate the formal living room. Instead, casual gatherings take place in the open-plan space that combines the family room, breakfast area, and large kitchen.

By contrast, the formal dining room is truly a showplace—and appropriately so, since it is the first room you see upon entering the home. The space includes a handsome coffered ceiling, rich hand-painted Regency-style chairs, a 90-inch custom dining table, and an elegant Italian chandelier with 22-carat gold detailing. French doors, topped with transoms in a diamond pattern, provide ocean views and lead to a screened porch. The same diamond-mullioned windows repeat in the family room, where a very traditional wing-back chair and other plush furnishings reside.

Opposite: A detached deck is a prime spot to take in ocean views. **Left:** Elegant French doors lead from the dining room to the enclosed porch. **Above:** Natural light brightens the beautiful master bath.

Old-World style commingles with modern conveniences in the kitchen. Buttery-yellow cabinets are adorned with a combination of paneled and glass-front doors to lend traditional flavor to the space. Still, a built-in microwave and a spot for a small TV were custom fitted to the cabinetry. Recessed into a cozy alcove is the six-burner stove, attended by a pot-filler and a handsome tiled back-splash. Old-fashioned shutters on the windows above the sink close for privacy, while transoms allow natural light to enter the space. One of the most family-friendly features in the kitchen is the central island. Measuring 11-feet long, it offers plenty of prep space for big meals and room for wooden bar stools to be pulled up for quick breakfasts or snacks. Other modern conveniences include two refrigerators, two dishwashers, and a walk-in pantry. And visible from the kitchen is a playroom for the owners' grandchildren.

The master suite conveys the same traditional style found in the rest of the home, yet its soothing tones afford a relaxing ambience. Another delight in the house is the wine cellar, set beneath the staircase. Finally, a screened porch with a fireplace—the husband's favorite room—is the perfect spot to enjoy the ocean views, even on cooler days.

Well-planned features, such as the built-in microwave and a pot-filler, give this old-fashioned kitchen a modern appeal. Left: The combined breakfast area and living room is relaxed and conversational.

A fireplace allows four-season use of the enclosed porch. **Right:** Set neatly behind the classically styled staircase is the much-loved wine room.

Well-placed palms line the modern-day
Plantation home in Winter Park, Florida.

Southern
Charm

In contrast to the easy-going architecture of beach-front houses you might find in the northeast, southern houses assume an air of grandeur and have a strong connection to the history of the region. Typically found in Georgia, Mississippi, Louisiana, and Florida, Plantation-style homes, referred to as "antebellum" homes, gained popularity approximately 30 years before the Civil War. Pillared front porches, dramatic entryways, grand staircases, and formal living spaces characterize this genre. In general, the design elements of Plantation houses stem from a mélange of styles from Classical Revival to Greek Revival to Federal.

Case in point is the Winter Park, Florida, house pictured here. The front of the home features a centered gable above a covered porch with slender, square columns, which are details seen in Colonial Revival architecture. The more unusual second-story porch emphasizes the tall stature of the design—a characteristic of many old southern houses that had to be built well above ground in order to protect the structures from flooding and excess moisture.

Spanning 11,000 square feet, this house is larger and less symmetrical than a classically designed Plantation home. Designing for a family with five children, Chris Peterson, the homeowner and a builder, and Charles Clayton III, of Charles Clayton Construction,

Opposite: Robust mouldings emphasize the entry door. **Left:** Brick is used around the fireplace as well as on the floor. **Above:** A decorative ceiling elevates the tone of the dining room.

created a layout that would work well for his large family. First of all, Chris and Wendi Peterson strongly felt that the design of the kitchen should start with an oversized island. Topped with blue granite from Afghanistan, the island was given a traditional flavor by being crafted to look like a piece of furniture. The large unit is made of pine and includes classic-style panels and English "bun" feet—also called "ball" feet, found on period furnishings from as far back as the 1700s.

A number of other details in the kitchen lend the home old-fashioned appeal. White cabinets have a simple panel design and drawers feature half-moon pulls. Exposed beams on the ceilings, the brick hearth, and a brick-patterned floor offer the interior warmth and rusticity while a unique quilt-like tile backsplash provides a touch of whimsy. With such a large family, it's not surprising to see many modern conveniences incorporated into the space, such as two sinks, a professional-grade range, and two wall ovens. Additionally, a full-sized refrigerator, full-sized freezer, as well as refrigerator drawers give the homeowners plenty of storage space for family dinners.

Adjacent to the kitchen is a family room and casual eating area. The everyday dining space features classic Roman shades on the windows and round-back chairs with turned legs reminiscent of those made in 18th-Century England. The family room includes comfortable furnishings that have a classic look, yet a relaxed feel. In contrast, the formal living room conveys Old World elegance. French doors lead into the space, where highly-detailed built-ins surround a brick fireplace, fine fabrics cover the traditional-style chairs, and an antique rug is underfoot.

Finally, the master suite combines history with comfort. A claw-foot tub is the highlight of the oversized bathroom and small octagonal tiles offer texture to the white floor. With all the careful planning and the fine craftsmanship, this new house recreates the feeling of a home from America's deep past.

Right: Playful tiles and a complementing island surface bring whimsy to the kitchen. **Opposite Above:** A colorful under-mounted prep sink is a delightful detail. **Opposite Below:** Garden views are available from the well-lit breakfast area.

Left: In the master bedroom, French doors open onto exclusive views of the garden. Above: Octagonal tiles and a mosaic "rug" are true Floridian details.

Classic symmetry, entry columns, and a fanlight define
this home in the Georgian Colonial style.

Fit for
a King

For its very regal stature, the Georgian style was named after the British kings that held power when such architecture became popular. From 1714 to 1820, King George I, George II, and George III ruled England. Georgian, a type of Colonial house, includes many classic elements that were derived from Italian Renaissance and Baroque forms. But unlike Renaissance structures of the late 15th and 16th Centuries and Baroque designs of the early 17th Century, Georgian homes offered a simpler appearance than its ornate predecessors.

Like most new houses, this one, created by William E. Poole Designs, Inc., combines elements from a variety of traditional styles. Starting with its perfectly symmetrical facade and fan-shaped window above the door—features characteristic of the Georgian style—and incorporating a Greek Revival-style entry outfitted with Ionic columns and a full-width porch, the Colonial has a classic, yet unique, appearance.

The 5,387 square-foot house includes four bedrooms, five baths, a powder room, as well as a gourmet kitchen, recreation room, and finished basement. A three-car garage is set neatly out of view in the back and breaks the symmetry of the house.

Walking into the house, you notice how the sunlight from the fanlights and transoms washes the foyer with a warm glow. A staircase with delicate wood balustrades encircles the foyer and leads to the second level. To give the interior an open feeling, columns in lieu of

Left: A formal foyer makes a noteworthy impression on visitors.
Below: Ionic columns loosely define the dining room from the foyer.

TRADITIONAL ELEGANCE

Historical Note

Georgian architecture became widespread in both England and America, although the English included more elaborate exterior details. For example, an English Georgian home might have had oversized steps and a large pediment with columns beneath, while an American Georgian house typically had a more modestly scaled overhang and, often, pilasters—half columns attached to the wall of the house, rather than standing freely like a true column. In the 18th Century, columns were predominantly made of stone; thus, they were expensive to build. Pilasters quickly became an affordable solution. The faux columns added a similar vertical element to the home at a fraction of the cost.

walls separate the foyer from the dining and living room. Just as on the exterior, the columns are in the Ionic order.

In the living room, high ceilings continue the open and airy feeling of the otherwise traditional structure. Light-hued furnishings offer plenty of seating, and French doors open to a terrace area with a trellis above. The house includes both a formal dining room as well as a casual breakfast nook with a charming bay window. Next to the breakfast area is a keeping room that affords an informal spot to relax. The wood-beamed ceiling gives it a more rustic look, unlike the other rooms in the house. The master bedroom and a library can be found on the first floor, while the other bedrooms and the recreation room are upstairs. The combination of the traditional forms and features and the designer's use of changing ceiling heights and open spaces make the house feel like a home.

Defining columns along the great room and dining room add an important historical element to the interior.

This home is native to New England, where
shingles and gambrels are in tradition.

New England
Classic

*A*rchitectural historian Vincent Scully popularized the term "shingle style" in the 1950s. The type of home, however, dates from the late 19th Century and stems from three architectural periods: Queen Anne (1880–1910), Colonial Revival (1880–1955), and Richardsonian Romanesque (1880–1900). Shingle-style houses, named for the thinly cut cedar that sheathed the exteriors, were first seen as vacation retreats on the New England coast.

A fine example is this Massachusetts home, designed for a couple from New Orleans. Its exterior clearly highlights the simple yet elegant forms found on the original Shingle-style homes. The gambrel roof, adapted from the Colonial Revival style, and the asymmetrical design are often found in both Queen Anne and Richardsonian Romanesque houses. The eyebrow dormer, which pops up just above the entry and adds a touch of whimsy to the traditional home, is typical of the Shingle style as well as the Richardsonian Romanesque look.

In addition to the eyebrow, the house includes plenty of classic multipaned windows to bring light inside. With the help of architect Mark Schmid of Cambridge, Massachusetts, and landscaped designer Raymond Thayer, the homeowners created a welcoming exterior for both the main house and the adjacent carriage house. (The carriage house was built first, so that the Louisiana-based owners had a place to stay while overseeing the construction of the main house.) Terraced gardens complement the handsome shingled structures. And once inside, the old-fashioned feeling continues with plenty of salvaged materials—but many practical elements are included to give the house a modern sensibility.

Above: Attention to details, such as the carvings on this mantel from Philadelphia, give the home its character. **Right:** Minimalist rustic furnishings keep rooms in tune with the design of the house.

Twenty-seven out of the twenty-eight paneled doors of the house were salvaged from old structures; worn out by salvage shopping, the owners admitted one new door, for a closet. Although the doors themselves are old, wide entryways are graciously sized and rooms flow easily into one another.

Wood beams extend from the living room to the dining room to effect a rustic flavor and promote a continuous feeling. In both rooms, the owners carefully selected the details. In the living room, for instance, an antique hand-carved mantelpiece from Philadelphia plays center stage, dramatizing architectural interest and elegant craftsmanship. Furnishings are kept simple to give the room a relaxed comfortable feeling, and a series of floor-to-ceiling French doors give access to the gardens beyond. The dining room includes an ornate 18th-Century French chandelier that hangs gracefully above the round table. Although the chandelier is made to hold wax candles, the unit now uses electric bulbs and wiring, encased within the hollowed-out candles.

Below: Buttery-yellow walls reflect a warm glow throughout the dining room and kitchen.
Opposite: Nearly every door in the home was salvaged from historical structures.

Modern stainless-steel appliances equip the sunny kitchen.

Historical Note

Dormers, first created in the early 1600s, have an interesting history. Derived from the French word *dormir*, which means to sleep, these windowed features were developed in order to transform attics into sleeping areas. They brought in light and ventilation to the upper rooms of a home long before the invention of light bulbs and forced-air systems.

A palette of warm tones is found throughout the home. A buttery-yellow graces the walls of both the kitchen and dining room, where resawn pine flooring also provides warmth. The boards were shipped from Louisiana to Massachusetts well before they were installed, because builder Ed Howland suggested that the wood should acclimate to the cooler temperatures of New England. This proved to be a good decision, since the owners have not had any problems with the floors. Other traditional elements in the kitchen include the bead-board siding on the island and the combination of paneled and windowed cabinets; yet granite counters and the stainless steel appliances remind us that this is a modern-day house—for homeowners with modern needs.

The private spaces have a similar atmosphere to the public areas—an air of comfort and tradition. The master bedroom, for instance, has beamed ceilings and French doors, but is set apart from the other rooms by its beautiful multipaned oval window. This type of window was often found in high-style Early Classical Revival homes, and it gives an air of distinction to both the exterior and interior of the house. The pairing of salvaged materials and classic features certainly takes this house from ordinary to extraordinary.

Gingerbread details and custom craftwork embellish the exterior in Victorian style. A dusty pink color scheme was also a historically informed choice.

True
Romance

*N*amed after Queen Victoria, who ruled Great Britain from 1837 to 1901, the Victorian style became popular in both England and America during the latter part of the queen's reign. The Victorian era engendered a number of styles: Second Empire, Queen Anne, Richardsonian Romanesque, Carpenter Gothic, Stick, and Shingle.

The house shown here and on the following pages includes elements that are reminiscent of the Queen Anne and Carpenter Gothic styles. Of the Victorian houses, Queen Annes are the most feminine and lavish, often including such features as bay windows, towers, delicate spindlework, one-story porches, and roof cresting (the railing on top of the roof). An architect named Richard Norman Shaw and a group of his contemporaries popularized the flamboyant style during the 1880s and 1890s, when the Industrial Revolution was in full force and mass production helped architects create elaborate forms without the high-cost labor of artisan craftsman.

Carpenter Gothic, which is the other Victorian substyle seen here, extends from Gothic Revival architecture. Gothic Revival includes both masonry and wood-frame construction, but Carpenter Gothic refers to solely the wooden structures made by, of course, carpenters. The carpenters of the period crafted ornate wooden details, which now typify what we know as Gingerbread houses. On this house, designed by Jerold Axelrod & Associates, we see the scrolling gingerbread trim along the edges of the windows.

Stenciling was a popular wall treatment in Victorian homes.

19th-Century details abound, including the moulded mantel and tiled fireplace surround.

Because the exterior architecture includes unusual elements like the towers and undulating forms, the interiors are very dynamic. Within the 2,696 square-foot structure, rooms are compact and have been decorated to reinforce the Victorian style. For instance, on either side of the entry foyer sit two odd-shaped spaces. The homeowners chose to have a media/guest room and the dining room in those areas. Light floods the dining room space through the five large windows. A delicate motif lines the wall where it meets the ceiling and continues on to provide visual interest. Lace draperies, often found in Victorian homes, and an 18th-Century Chippendale-style chair give the rounded dining space its traditional flavor.

Although this house does not have a formal living room, the great room, which is located just off the kitchen on the first floor, offers classic elegance. The vaulted ceiling sets the great room apart from the other rooms in the house. A beautifully detailed fireplace can be enjoyed while the homeowners are in the great room, the breakfast area, or the kitchen.

Above Left: A turret distinguishes the home's Victorian style and houses a formal dining room. **Right:** Colorful craftsmanship adorns the front door and pediment above the entrance.

French doors to the rear deck brighten the great room. **Opposite:** An open layout between the great room and kitchen invites easy entertaining.

The kitchen is probably the most simply designed room of the house, but it has a very functional layout and timeless materials. An island is set on a diagonal to separate the cooking area from the casual dining space. This layout provides easy access for the chef to bring meals to the table and allows him or her to entertain guests while preparing food.

Also on the first floor is the master bedroom, which has a tray ceiling, the master bath, another full bathroom, and laundry area. The well-designed layout proves that although the Victorian structure does not feature oversized rooms, an efficient use of space can provide comfortable living areas. Upstairs, three more bedrooms and a bath reside. Finally, a recreation room, which is part of the tower over the media space below, features a stunning domed ceiling. With such rich details, it's easy to see why homeowners are drawn to the charm of a 19th-Century-style home.

A wide porch spans the many
entrances to the front of the house.

Grand *Plans*

For a 15,000 square-foot house in a coastal town in New Jersey, Bay Head architect John Lederer took a contemporary approach to classic Shingle-style architecture. With cedar shingles on the sides and the roof, the house immediately gives the impression of an abode that might have been built in the late 1800s. Additionally, if you look closely, you'll see that the shingled walls run without interruption at the corners—another feature characteristic of the Shingle style. The hipped roof, with its sloping ends, and side gables further promote the traditional feeling. Typical elaborations of the 19th-Cenury versions, which are also found on this New Jersey home, include ranks of three or more windows in a row, Palladian windows, extensive porches, and towers.

Due to the large size of this house, the architect took care in creating a structure that didn't appear overbearing. Incorporating towers and varying the roofline bring visual interest to the exterior and allow for intimate spaces. On the whole, the rooms are quite large while having a warm, welcoming atmosphere. From the front entrance, you can see straight out to the backyard through a series of French doors. Four columns gracefully separate the foyer from the living room. In the forefront, a double stairway creates a dramatic statement and frames the living room. Made with cherry treads and handrails to contrast the white painted balusters, the stairway even includes molding beneath, so that it is attractive when one is standing on the first floor looking up.

The foyer's sense of grandeur comes from a
marble floor inlaid with a compass circle and
ceremonial stairway.

A bridge from the guest suite to the rest of the house
creates an arched focal point to a rear courtyard.

TRADITIONAL ELEGANCE

For the interiors, the homeowners turned to Shrewsbury interior designer Suzette Donleavy for assistance. Donleavy strived to put together what she calls a "relaxed traditional environment." There are several living spaces—a formal living room, a hearth room, a game room, and a family room—in order to accommodate the big family and their guests. (In the past, the owners have hosted up to 25 family members overnight.) Each of the living spaces offers old-fashioned appeal. Some of the highlights of the spaces include 20-foot ceilings in the hearth room, stained-glass windows with a family crest in the game room, and scalloped-edge built-in bookcases in the family room.

Like the other rooms, the kitchen affords a sense of grandeur and distinction. Designed by Leonardis Kitchen Interiors, of Morristown, the space works as beautifully as it looks. A handsome, oversized island with furniture-like detailing, such as paneled sides and carved brackets, is topped with a richly hued granite

Opposite: Transom windows with diamond-shaped panes help add even more light to the 20-foot-tall hearth room. **Left:** Tall windows brighten the living room, reserved for formal gatherings. **Above:** Oak floors and ceiling beams in a carriage-wheel pattern set off the breakfast room.

A granite-topped island with paneled base and carved brackets lends age-old elegance to the kitchen.

Above: A work station in the kitchen, complete with internet access, provides a convenient place for doing housework.

counter. Two elegant chandeliers hang above the island and supplement both recessed and under-cabinet lighting in the large kitchen. A porcelain farmhouse sink lends charm, while the six-burner cooktop offers plenty of firepower for preparing a meal for a big group. The refrigerator blends in neatly with the cabinetry since it is crafted with paneled doors to match the storage units. In addition to the high-performance appliances and fixtures in the kitchen, an outdoor bar area also has a refrigerator, a sink, and a television.

For the private spaces, Donleavy used the same warm neutral palette that can be seen throughout the house. Plush seating areas fill the space from the main house to the guest house, set above the garage. Detailed custom woodwork, luxurious window treatments, and properly-scaled (large enough to fill the grand rooms) traditional furnishings give all the rooms a rich ambiance. All the carefully selected elements work well together and the homeowners got exactly what they wanted: a spacious house that feels like it has been around for over 100 years.

Wood shingle siding and decorative columns
surround the 4,700 square-foot home.

Focus on *Family*

The differences between today's new homes and those from the past manifest themselves in practical features. Here, for instance, a wood shingle home lined with decorative columns and multipaned windows has a welcoming, traditional ambience inside and out. But the firm of Alan Mascord Design Associates, Inc., which has offices in Oregon and Washington state, also incorporated modern elements to promote easy living for a family. The 4,790-square-foot house includes four bedrooms, five full baths, and a half bath. Having more bathrooms than bedrooms is certainly rare in older homes, but for new houses, it's just one of the many amenities included to make life a little simpler, especially for families with children.

Unlike the days when only the cooking staff used it, the kitchen of a modern home is central to everyday family life. Seen here, the all-important island affords the kitchen an old-fashioned flavor with a marble counter, paneled doors, and half-moon cabinet pulls; but its scale and shape are contemporary. The lower portion of the unit is used to prepare foods, while the higher curved section makes a place for meals on the go. Wide walkways around the island help multiple chefs work simultaneously or when family members are in the kitchen together. The nearby breakfast nook is set in a windowed alcove adjacent to the cooking space and has plenty of seating for guests.

Dual under-mounted sinks built into the center island, plus loads of cabinets and counters, cater to serious cooks. **Right:** Wood floors and surrounding views of the landscape bring a country feel to the kitchen.

Above: Immediate access to the veranda from the kitchen enables large-scale entertaining.
Right: The second-floor landing overlooks the comfortable great room below.
Opposite: A built-in hutch displays china in the formal dining room.

Next to the kitchen is a vaulted great room, measuring approximately 30 by 20 feet. Due to its size, this space is great for entertaining. Plush furnishings are classic in style, but not too stuffy, which creates a very casual, comfortable feeling for the room. French doors open to a veranda, giving homeowners the option to expand their entertaining space beyond the interior rooms. On the opposite side of the kitchen, a mudroom leads to the four-car garage. Again, the large garage is not typical of older homes, but definitely provides the convenience that a growing family with friends would need.

The master bedroom takes in panoramic
views of the surrounding property.

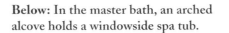
Below: In the master bath, an arched alcove holds a windowside spa tub.

TRADITIONAL ELEGANCE

The foyer, with its coffered ceiling; the office that includes a paneled built-in desk area; and the elegant dining room have a more formal feeling than the great room and kitchen. The master suite, located on the first floor, lends the home both comfort and sophistication. A box-bay window has a fanlight transom above, bringing in plenty of natural light. A similar window is found in the guest room, also on the first level. A crisp, clean-lined fireplace and access to a private veranda are just a few of the special elements that homeowners will enjoy. His-and-her closets and master baths make the morning rush a breeze. A shower with dual heads links the couple's bathrooms; one gets the benefit of a spa tub tucked into a windowed alcove. Finally, upstairs placement of the two bedrooms, two baths, and a media/playroom for the kids lets the owners reclaim peace and quiet—certainly a luxury that transcends time.

A built-in desk helps the office stay spacious.
Opposite: Windows surround the sitting
area in the main-level guest room.

EUROPEAN INFLUENCE

From the shores of the Mediterranean to Great Britain, Europe's beautiful homes and rich history continue to influence American architects. And why not? It's hard to resist the seaside designs that have an open, airy atmosphere or the regal inland structures that include plenty of detail and elegant materials. For example, a 16,000-square-foot Long Island home gets its rich flavor from the work of well-known British architect Sir Edwin Lutyens. A separate wing houses an indoor pool inspired by structures built during turn-of-the-century England. You'll also find homes with such details as the red-tile roofs of Italian villas. For a taste of Spanish-American culture, visit a 13,000 square-foot hacienda in Paradise Valley, Arizona, first envisioned by the owner and architect during a trip to Guadalajara.

When architecture is kin to the land, environmentally and socially responsible building methods are doubly appropriate. Read about the Florida home built by the National Association of Home Builders with sustainable materials, features for energy efficiency, and access for the disabled.

In the yard, a child's swing fashioned as an airplane offers a touch of whimsy to the 15-acre site.

English *Accent*

Built for a true Anglophile, his wife, and four children, this Long Island home includes an abundance of original details from both the U.S. and across the pond. To create the owners' dream house, the couple hired East Hampton, New York, architect Douglas Moyer. Moyer truly enjoyed working with the homeowners, because they were so involved in the project. The husband often sketched ideas and showed Moyer examples of architecture that he admired. The result of their efforts is the transformation of a simple 1,200 square-foot shelter with rough-sawn cedar siding to a spectacular 12,000 square-foot house with beautiful architectural and decorative features reminiscent of those found in English country houses.

As an admirer of famed 20th-Century British architect Sir Edwin Lutyens, the homeowner selected materials that were similar to those used in Lutyens' works. For example, stonework plays an important part in the design of the home: Connecticut green stone, topped with bluestone, is used on the foundation of the house, giving the structure a stately appearance. Reclaimed bricks on the chimneys and antique oak interior doors with line-fold carvings (a European technique that dates from the late 1600s) lend the home authentic Old World style. Additionally, many leaded and stained-glass windows—which were popular with English glassmakers—frame the views of the 15-acre property. The geometric arrangement of the window panes—five panes wide at the top, then four wide, then three and two—symbolizes the tree of life, according to the homeowner.

Opposite: Custom sidelights flank the front door and illuminate the foyer. **Above:** The second-floor hallway is dressed with oak, walnut, and cherry woods.

Honey-toned white oak woodwork is found in all the rooms and creates a welcoming atmosphere in the grand abode. The entry way has a graceful wood-framed door with custom side lights created by a local craftsman and based on the owner and architect's drawings. Matching details are found on the mouldings that surround the bookshelves of the library, reading room, and office. The spaces are separated from each other by pocket doors topped with transoms. Wood-paneled walls lend character to the otherwise simple dining room. In the nearby butler's pantry, custom cabinetry shows off the natural grain of the oak.

Behind doors, a butler's pantry is on call with storage, bar sink, and cooler.

Opposite and Above: Pale-hued subway tiles, Carrara marble counters, and top-of-the-line appliances make the kitchen a showstopper. A half-moon circle lends a romantic touch.

This Page and Opposite: Formerly located outside the home, the 60-foot pool now occupies its own wing of the house and is available year-round.

By contrast, the kitchen is sparse in its use of wood tones, seen only on the oversized hutch with drawers and the breakfast dining table and chairs. In lieu of wood, classic light-colored subway tiles line the walls and add texture to the space. Matching marble forms the counters and sink. Two arched windows—one in the cleanup area and the other in the breakfast room—become focal points of the space. Of course, a well-crafted kitchen with simple European flavor should include high-performance appliances, such as the Aga and Viking stoves. A flat-screen TV, also a modern amenity, is wall-mounted to preserve counter space.

Finally, a truly unique and stunning feature of the house is the 60-foot indoor pool. Moyer lined the space with stone and tiles—a nod to Lutyens' style. Originally, the pool was outside the home, but desiring more opportunities to use it, the owners enclosed the pool and attached it to the house. Surrounded by multi-paned arched windows and transoms, swimmers can enjoy the views of the outdoors throughout the year.

The home approaches the street with a
generous amount of period details, such as
the carved trim surrounding the entry.

A Foreign *Affair*

*O*riginating in countries north of the Mediterranean Sea, such as Italy, Greece, and Spain, Mediterranean-style architecture offers a distinct look. Popular in the late 1800s and early 1900s, the style's features directly reflect their beachfront location. The colors mimic the surrounding landscape with cool watery blues and earthy neutrals. Think painted walls and terracotta tiles. And the design of these houses accommodates the warm climate of the Mediterranean. Open planning, for example, allow for views and ventilation.

Here, the American adaptation of a Mediterranean home includes plenty of Old World details. Artfully created by Bill and Greg Weber, an undulating low-pitched Spanish tile roof lends European flavor at first sight. The brackets set beneath the roof extend from the ornate detailing found on Italian Renaissance houses built from 1890 to 1915. And the arched windows remind us of those found on villas overlooking the sea. To modernize the turn-of-the-century style, the designer included a series of windows gracefully stepping upwards on the colonnade portion of the facade.

Although the house is over 8,000 square feet, there is a sense of warmth that pervades the spaces. For instance, when you walk into the home, cheerful-hued walls in a sunny yellow—a color that's often used in Mediterranean homes—greet you in the foyer. Large tile stone floors are scaled perfectly to fit the gracious space, and the stone continues up the stairs. Niches carved out of the walls give homeowners a place to display their treasures, while an elegant chandelier illuminates the entry.

The entry leads to a double-height parlor. For architectural interest, columns separate the parlor from the dining room space, and are also used on the top floor, which can be seen from the parlor. Comfortable furnishings with a distinct European flavor are upholstered in warm yellows and accessorized with bronze and burnt-orange pillows. The stunning room also includes a handsome fireplace and tall windows that face the water beyond. The family room includes a more muted color palette, and offers a casual place to sit and enjoy the views. Set next to the lanai, this space is great for entertaining when the weather allows.

On the other side of the family room is the kitchen. Two islands serve different purposes. The central one can be used for preparing dinners or lunches, while the other offers a place for meals on the go. Both have handy prep sinks. Wood cabinetry features furniture-like detailing, and a matching built-in wall unit holds a high-tech entertainment system.

The foyer showcases the dramatic sweep of the central stairway. **Opposite:** The kitchen's lighting plan includes recessed fixtures, decorative pendants, and a chandelier.

Above: Interior spaces zoned for public use are unified by the outdoor living areas at the back of the home. The result is a resort-like ambiance, perfect for this coastal setting.

For dining spaces, the house features a charming breakfast nook with a circular ceiling above and a curved window with water views, as well as a dramatic formal dining room. The two-story-high space showcases a decorative ceiling with a unique finish. Plush draperies, a crystal chandelier, and an Oriental rug finish the look. The dining table comfortably seats 10 guests with plenty of room to walk around the table.

In terms of private areas, the house has five bedrooms. The master suite is on the main floor, which gives the homeowners privacy when they have guests upstairs. The bedrooms are all elegantly decorated and are oriented to take advantage of the lovely views. The master has access to the outdoors via a long terrace. With the European detailing, the combination of both formal and casual rooms, plus the truly luxurious exterior space, this well-planned house is one that can be appreciated on the shores of the Mediterranean as well as in the States.

Classically styled furnishings occasion a comfortable conversation area around the great room's fireplace.

Finely cultivated grounds set the tone
for the elegant European-style home.

A Taste of
Tuscany

Inspired by the wonderfully elegant homes set in the hillside towns of Italy, homeowners and avid travelers Barbara and Mike Ruddy created their own 6,500 square-foot retreat to include plenty of European flavor. To start, Mike, who acted as the home's chief designer, crafted an L-shaped plan reminiscent of how Tuscan villas are often laid out. A circular driveway and the arch motif, used for the windows, French doors, and garage doors, reinforce the open, welcoming quality of Tuscan architecture. This house, however, is located in Georgia's Skidaway Island, a picturesque interior barrier island just south of historic Savannah. The Italian style suits the location quite well. For instance, the Mediterranean-style wraparound covered verandas—all equipped with ceiling fans—comfort the owners during the hottest of Georgian summers. Graceful archways frame verdant views of the surrounding marshes just as well as they would the hills of the Tuscan countryside.

Upon entering the home, the formal foyer gives visitors a sense of the grandeur to come. A dramatic chandelier hangs from a recessed circular niche in the tray ceiling and shiny marble lines the floor. A series of columns—some of which are structural and some purely decorative—defines the space. Savannah artist Kipling Collins painted faux finishes on the walls to make them resemble aged frescos. The detail is straight out of Tuscan villas built hundreds of years ago.

Opposite: Handsome columns gently define rooms. **Above:** Arches and colonnades enclose this excellent seasonal space, great for entertaining.

Throughout the home, Barbara showcases the art and furnishings she collected from all over the globe during her career at the World Bank. The living room is filled with such treasures, elevating the space with special distinction. Above the mantel is a 300-year-old mirror from France, and an Indian sari adorns the coffee table. The dining room, which features 16-foot ceilings, displays Barbara's collection of rich-hued Italian fabrics. Woven draperies and panels hang from ceiling to floor to make the space feel even taller, and a pleated Roman shade provides another layer of luxury. On the dining room table is the pièce de résistance: a patchwork of Florentine fabrics hand-selected by Barbara from a shop that opened the 1500s. Gold trim with tassels finishes the beautiful table covering. The dining chairs feature a complementary fabric, and a gilded niche that holds an antique vase punctuates the red walls. The result is a dramatic dining space that the homeowners adore.

Opposite: Treasured collectibles find their place on the shelves of the study. **Left:** Sumptuous Italian fabrics soften and elevate the mood in the grand dining room. **Above:** A sculpted mantel matches the robust columns lining the formal living room.

The warming drawer built into the central island will find everyday use.

Below Left and Right: A star-studded motif and a burst of
color attract attention in the niche and family room.

EUROPEAN INFLUENCE

The kitchen, family room, and private spaces have a more relaxed feeling than the dining room. Honey-toned cabinets, oak floors, under-cabinet lighting, and a corner range hood all promote a feeling of warmth in the kitchen. The family room's casual ambiance is created with patterned transitional furnishings and a neutral palette, but the subtle décor is a backdrop to sculptures collected from all over the world. Influenced by a ceiling treatment in the Gregorian Egyptian Museum in the Vatican that Barbara loved, Kipling painted the ceiling with gold stars on a deep blue background. The same treatment extends to a niche in the hallway that holds African masks and statues. Last of all, the master suite offers soothing tones and an elevated style. The Renaissance-inspired painting on its wall is an appropriate final touch.

Opposite: A cooler palette brings calm to the master bedroom. **Below:** The master bath has a sunny, gardenside feel that's a pleasure to wake up to.

Situated in the Arizona desert, the 13,000 square-foot private home feels like a resort.

Paradise *Found*

*O*ften, the versions of Spanish architecture that we see in the U.S. fall into the category of either Spanish Colonial Revival or Spanish Eclectic and share elements that appear in Mission- and Pueblo-style houses. Here, architect Wes Balmer and builder Cal Christiansen, both from Phoenix, created this Paradise Valley, Arizona house to replicate a Mexican hacienda. They even took a week-long trip to Guadalajara, Mexico, to study the architecture, materials, and decorative features of the country. In the resulting design, beautiful pale tones of stucco walls, the texture of the red tile roof, and the welcoming quality of the arched openings all exude Spanish style.

Both the exteriors and interiors of the 13,000 square-foot desert home include features that are clearly inspired by Spanish architecture. The facade, for example, has a strong horizontal quality that is characteristic of houses you might find along the Mediterranean shoreline. The rounded tower and decorated chimney descend from Spanish Eclectic designs. And the back of the house includes a series of arched doorways, multilevel rooflines, fountains, and an oversized pool that makes the house feel like a resort.

Inside the sprawling abode, rooms connect via Pueblo-like archways. In the great room, 19-foot ceilings feature massive Douglas-fir beams 40-feet long. The beams were hand-picked for their size, then carved by craftsman. The room also boasts custom wood floors, made of hand-scraped wide-plank oak and stone. The size of the furnishings are the right scale for the grand space. Two chandeliers supplement the natural light that comes in from the windowed doors and transoms.

Above and Opposite: A traditionally minded courtyard and pool capture this home's affinity to nature. A judicious amount of landscaping, whimsical fountains, and careful lighting create outdoor "rooms" that are just as inviting as the rest of the design.

Above: Long lines of sight invite exploration of the layout. **Right:** Culturally loaded details in the kitchen reflect the taste and attitude of the owner. **Opposite:** Seasonal spaces like this sitting area allow the environment to enter the life of the home.

The focus of the kitchen is its central island. Meticulously designed by the architect, the island is adorned with ornate carvings. The surrounding cabinetry features the same level of detail on its paneled doors and trims. A large hearth is decorated with a tile backsplash and border design. Above it is a bull's head—certainly a nod to Spanish culture.

To connect the indoor living spaces with the outdoor courtyard, the architect and builder fashioned a massive wood-framed arch with a decorative transom window. The courtyard allows the homeowners to entertain year round and has plenty of comfortable seating and a fireplace.

It's clear to see that this house was a labor of love for Wes and Cal. There are so many beautiful details that were carefully planned and executed throughout the rooms. For instance, a delicate wrought-iron rail leads guests up the stairs in the rotunda. Once at the top, an elaborate chandelier hangs from a circular opening and carved brackets outline the ceiling space. A series of narrow windows lets light wash the rotunda. And just off of this foyer area are two guest suites, accessible by way of an additional entrance. The Spanish-style decor continues in the master and guest suites with such features as a heavily carved four-poster bed and Mission-style furnishings. Even the color palette throughout the rooms is typically Spanish, with red punctuating warm neutrals. The result is an Arizona home that offers comfortable, relaxed rooms, intricate carvings, rich materials, and plenty of foreign accents. The homeowner compares the house to having a dream resort—his own slice of paradise.

A familiar fireplace comforts this space and invites everyday family interaction. Left: Decorative brackets emphasize the shape and brightness of the second-floor landing.

A Team Effort

In order for a project to be successful (like this one was), you must hire a team of experts that you admire and trust. Here are some surefire tips to get the pros you need:

- **Call your friends and neighbors**: The best way to find a professional is asking your friends. If there's a house you like a few blocks away, see if you can contact the homeowners to find out the architect's and builder's names.

- **Interview carefully**: Your interview process should be two-fold. First, let the expert explain how he or she works. You'll want to see a portfolio of their work, get references, and find out what they expect in terms of payment. Second, be clear about what you're looking for. Describe the scope of the project, your budget, and your timeline.

- **Get references**: Call at least three people to find out if this person is reliable. Try to ask specific questions, such as "Is there anything so-and-so could improve upon?"

- **Put everything in writing**: A detailed contract will save you time and money. Make sure to spell out every detail including model numbers and specific materials to be used on the project. Include a dispute-resolution clause, so that if there is a problem, it can be handled in a timely, civil manner.

The Spanish Floridian exterior is appropriate
to the neighborhood. But this home's built-in
advantages are like none other on the block.

Smart
& *Stylish*

*B*uilt by a team of designers at the National Association of Home Builders, this cutting-edge Florida house combines elegant, classic features with modern design techniques that foreshadow the future of residential development in America. For instance, Spanish Floridian elements like the varied roofline and stucco exterior have been designed and built to exceed local hurricane-preparedness codes. This layout takes advantage of the surrounding views—the house is located on Lake Burden in Windermere, Florida—and exposes more interior spaces to natural light and cross breezes than a traditionally designed home. The house measures a more than comfortable 10,023 square feet on two levels and is close to 100-percent wheelchair accessible: an elevator services the second floor. In addition to these Universal Design features, the house is certified by the Florida Green Building Coalition Home Designation Standard. The house is estimated to save 45 percent more in whole-house heating costs than the average home, thanks to ultra-efficient doors and windows and carefully placed insulation. A HEPA air-filtration system and high-efficiency heat pumps also help to keep ideal temperatures in a six-zone system. In fact, the entire home is ENERGY STAR®-rated by the U.S. Department of Energy's "Building America" program.

Furthermore, materials like sustainable hardwood flooring, recycled mulch, and an aggregate veneer flagstone (an eco-friendly alternative to real stone) for the fireplace make the house "green." Even the gutter system was cleverly designed; rainwater is captured and used to irrigate the property, so that tap water is conserved.

Palm trees shade the pool during day. An outdoor warms the area at night. **Right:** A carefree seating area overlooks Lake Burden.

Above and Right: Sliding doors open out interior spaces and cool the home with cross breezes.

The palm-lined house is designed to not only be eco-friendly and well-planned for aging homeowners, but also to have a resort-like quality. An abundance of outdoor terraces, some with kitchens and fireplaces, allow owners to sit back and enjoy the warm Florida climate. There's also a dock for boats and a dramatic infinity-edge pool shaded by more planted palms.

Inside, gracious spaces pair luxurious materials with an easy-going ambiance. Making the large home feel cozy took some effort, according to interior designer Donald Saxon. The kitchen attains an overall sense of warmth with the honey-colored cabinets, textural ceiling, and carefully chosen pendant lighting. The cooking area gets a touch of European elegance with a massive range hood constructed of precast stone and cabinets decorated with corbels and spindles. A diamond-patterned backsplash creates a visual focal point and complements the color of the marble counters. Multiple sinks—including one in a deep apron style—and stainless-steel appliances offer modern convenience.

Other than the paneled walls and massive fireplace in family room, the casual-gathering spaces are relatively simple. Much of the family room furnishings do double duty. For example, ottomans can be used for additional seating or as small tables, perfect for setting down a cup of tea. Nesting tables come in handy when guests need a place to set down a drink or hors d'oeuvre. A smart feature in the family room: sliding glass doors give access to the adjacent loggia, doubling the living space.

Opposite: Conversation areas are scaled for intimacy.
Left: When every part of the home is one-room deep, even the kitchen receives first-row views. **Above:** Counter space and decorative elements are plentiful.

Classic details and rich materials adorn the private areas. In lieu of a head-board, panels and transom windows are set behind the bed in the master suite. Natural light beams in when the sun comes up. And since the windows are close to the ceiling, privacy is not an issue. For the bath, a variety of stones combine to give a luxurious look. A windowed tub provides a delightful place to relax in this opulent smart house.

The master bath is a picture of luxury amenities.
Opposite: The master bedroom was designed with furniture placement in mind.

Lushly landscaped grounds soften the angular
exterior of the European-style structure.

A Manor
Born

The term "manor house" dates back to the Middle Ages. Manors were generally rambling structures, created for the lords, of the Feudal system. Depending on the location, manors were fortified appropriately. Some had small windows in order to preserve the privacy and protect the lord o the house. Modern-day manors, like the 11,443-square-foot one shown here, of course, do not have the design restrictions in terms of safety as the ones from the Middle Ages, but do have the regal appearance of their predecessors.

At first glance, the limestone entry and front garden terrace gives one a sense of the stately quality that this house possesses, both inside and out. Copper dormers with rounded tops line the roof and emphasize the symmetry of the facade—all hallmarks of French Eclectic architecture. Resemblance also to Tudor homes is not accidental; Medieval English architecture had a strong influence in France, especially in the northern regions such as Normandy. The simple arched entryway is typical of the style's distaste for pretentious ornamentation.

Mike Studer, of Studer Residential Design, designed the elegant manor. The main floor, which is over 5,000 square feet, holds the main living areas as well as the master suite. All the living spaces are adorned with beautiful furnishings: upholstered pieces feature rich fabrics and case goods are made of fine woods. Heavy crown moldings define the ceilings, while paneling and chair rails grace the lower portion of some walls, like the one in the formal dining room. Many rooms feature such handsome details as medallions, paneling, and coffered ceilings.

Above Left: A ceiling medallion emphasizes the ornate chandelier. **Above Right:** A robust fireplace surround is in sharp contrast to the dark wood walls and ceiling.

A lighter palette informs the spacious kitchen. **Below Left:** Serious appliances and a working layout enables the family cook to impress.

The grand kitchen certainly looks like it belongs in a European manor house. The interesting finish and carvings on the cabinetry are in the Old World style, and the massive hearth creates a focal point in the room with its warm tile backsplash. Additionally, the inclusion of two islands makes the kitchen's layout stand out: one holds a prep sink and plenty of counter space; the other has a curved design and seats for casual dining or snacking.

Just off of the kitchen sits the breakfast nook and the hearth room, the latter of which showcases a fireplace with a very regal surround. In fact, this house has four fireplaces on the main floor—in the library, the great room, the master bedroom, and the hearth room—plus one in the lower-level rec room.

The great room showcases all the decorative detailing that can be found throughout the home.

Other interesting public spaces in the house include a dark wood-clad pub area, sunken porch and solarium, media room, exercise room, billiard room, and wine cellar. Eighteenth-Century style combines with 21st-Century technology in what architects refer to as the wine grotto: wrought-iron gates cover the built-in wine storage area, and a tavern-like sitting area lets homeowners enjoy their collection of reds and whites. In terms of private spaces, you'll find a master suite with views of the landscaped grounds through stately Palladian windows, an oversized master bath that has dressing area, and access to multiple walk-in closets. Three other bedrooms pamper family and guests in a fashion befitting a European manor.

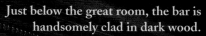
Just below the great room, the bar is handsomely clad in dark wood.

Top and Above: On the main level, the master suite has direct access to the sunken solarium—which, in turn, opens onto the sunken rear porch.

Especially dramatic at night, the home was
designed to be a mecca for entertaining.

Party
Planner

*A*rchitecture has always borrowed features from earlier trends and remote locations. Certainly, this Huntington Beach, California, house is no exception, blending European elements that are imbued with a Mediterranean flavor. Built for a couple who loves to entertain and has four children, the stately house was designed by architect David Pacheo of DPA Architecture in Huntington Beach. The homeowners wanted a place that was functional and fun, yet elegant, according to the wife. They also host about four large parties a year. And because the house would need to accommodate even more guests during the holidays, it would require a thoughtfully planned layout.

Curb appeal and first impressions are always important; but for this house, entertaining visitors would be top priority. With that in mind, Pacheo worked with the homeowners to create a dramatic entry. Flanked by planters and almost-sculptural trees, the 18-foot-high wrought-iron archway offers plenty of impact, incorporating scrollwork that you might find on houses bordering the Mediterranean Sea. Once inside, the drama continues: A double stair gracefully curves up to the mezzanine level and fans out to create balconies overlooking the elegant foyer. Dan Yadgir, the contractor on the project, worked closely with the husband in order to get the staircase just right. The owner had seen a handrail that he liked in a scene in the movie *The Matrix* that he showed to Yadgir for inspiration.

The fireplace and media center
offer two reasons to linger in
the family room. Opposite:
The kitchen makes good use of
European country details.

For the interiors, the homeowners enlisted Margo Hazlett to work in conjunction with the other pros. Hazlett had worked with the homeowners for two other residences, so she knew just what they were looking for. Throughout the rooms, a deep neutral color palette of bronzes, creams, crimsons, and chocolates pervades and offers richness without dominating the spaces. Although the consistent tones visually unify the rooms, each exhibits its own distinct personality. For example, each space features a unique ceiling treatment. The husband wanted his guests to be able to look up and be surprised at the disparate treatments above their heads. In one of the two kitchens dual cooking areas makes entertaining a breeze, intricately hand-carved beam supports provide visual interest. And hung from the decorative ceiling is a light fixture that complements the heavy design above. The oversized electric "candelabra" brightens the island and stands out as an important design element in the room. Also in the room is an ornately detailed range hood that exudes European elegance. And mosaic tiles in tones of beige and burnt sienna conjure details one might find in an Italian villa.

For a touch of Spanish flavor, look to the fireplace in the living room. Its intricate carvings and dark color create a visual focal point in the room. Also in the room is an eight-foot long two-sided sofa, which allows guests to face either the handsome fireplace or the views of the canal outside.

The outdoor space is prime for entertaining. The backyard is twice as large as that of the owners' previous property. In fact, the back terraces boast seating that accommodates 120 people. And with two outdoor fireplaces and a waterfall-edged pool, family and guests often end up outdoors even though the indoor spaces are equally spectacular. The whole project took three years to complete, but the homeowners feel that the time was definitely well spent.

Hooded arches and richly textured
stucco finish adorn the facade.

Roman *Holiday*

The Renaissance Period, a time of "rebirth" (the direct translation of the word), spanned from the 14th to the 16th Century. Artists in fields like literature, art, and architecture took a new, more inspired look at their craft and refined it. Michelangelo, Da Vinci, and Palladio were just a few of the famous artisans during this time. Later, in the 1800s, a revival period of Italian Renaissance architecture began with its principles rooted in the original Renaissance designs. Features like a hipped roof with projecting wings, a symmetrical facade, an arched entry are all elements that were found in Italian Renaissance architecture from the late 19th Century—as captured in the house shown here.

Reminiscent of a Mediterranean-style villa, the 4,588 square-foot home has four bedrooms and four and a half baths. Created by Dan F. Sater, the exterior of the home is inviting and impressive. Scrolling ironwork greets visitors at the front door, and a complementary pattern is inlaid on the stone floor. The elegant foyer is flanked by a formal dining room—outfitted with heavy wood furnishings, a traditional tapestry hung on the wall, and a delicate chandelier with a leaf motif—and the study. In contrast to the intimate scale of these rooms, the great room measures approximately 23 by 22 feet and has a dramatic vaulted ceiling soaring above. The focal point of the great room is a wall of built-ins centered on a space for a flatscreen television. Here, technology, albeit on display, is camouflaged by the beautiful paneled woodwork and graceful arched molding that highlights the area. Plush seating and plenty of tables makes entertaining in the room very enjoyable. Throughout the living areas, beamed ceilings offer another layer of visual interest to the spaces.

The kitchen affords a Tuscan flavor. The detailed cabinetry, a unique tile backsplash, and the carved range hood remind us of cooking spaces found in the hillside homes of Tuscany. A deep reddish hue covers the walls while a basic beige color graces the floors. The kitchen includes a breakfast nook that faces the verandah beyond, where a second kitchen is located. The covered cooking area has the same rich qualities as the primary kitchen with an artfully crafted backsplash and a handsome range hood. Sitting poolside or in the columned gazebo area, friends and family can enjoy dining alfresco during the day and even into the evening.

A favorite area of the house is the master suite. Located in its own wing, the master suite features a dramatic shape, so that windows can curve around both the bedroom and bath areas to take advantage of the views. The master bedroom faces the verandah and the bath looks out onto a private garden in the front of the house. Luxury abounds in the master bath with its circular spa-like tub, elegant wood cabinetry, and decorative wall coverings. Three guest suites—one of which is located by itself on the second floor—all have walk-in closets and are beautifully decorated. Certainly, family and guests all welcome the resort-like feeling that this house has to offer.

Opposite: Efficiency guided the layout of the kitchen. But the backsplash and hood were designed for style. **Left:** A robust fireplace anchors this seasonal sitting area. **Above:** The master bath offers the experience of a private spa.

RUSTIC RETREATS

Whether they're lakeside getaways among the trees or a mountaintop chalet, these rough-hewn structures have never gone out of style. Before the railroad was built, American colonists had to use the materials at hand. During the 17th Century, lumber was a plentiful commodity and worked well as building material—thus, the log cabin trend was born. Since then, the simple cabin has come a along way. They now include all the amenities—proper plumbing, ventilation systems, and modern appliances and fixtures—of a modern home and reflect exciting advances in residential building that enhance the natural beauty of log construction. For instance, instead of clearing the nearest forest for lumber, one builder carefully selected "standing dead" trees that would take minimal processing and had them delivered to the remote job site. But such pains were quickly forgotten by the crew as, log by log, the 10,000 square-foot home rose out of the picturesque mountains overlooking Lake Tahoe.

Views like this are what led the owners to build this log home.

Standing *Strong*

The history of the American log home dates back to the first European settlements in North America. In the regions that would become the middle colonies, such as New Jersey, Pennsylvania, Delaware, and Maryland, settlers combined the local availability of lumber and their native know-how of building techniques to erect the first American log homes. Constructed of horizontally placed log walls held together by an interlocking or notching system, the massive walls of the early homes were extremely strong; in fact, many original homes are still intact. The log home's durability, as well as its ability to showcase fine craftsmanship and natural beauty of exposed wood, still appeals to many homeowners.

In an effort to create an updated and elegant log cabin, the owners and architect Sherry Guzzi spent three years building the 10,000-square-foot structure set on 16 acres of land overlooking Lake Tahoe. Conscious of the beautiful surroundings, the homeowner selected builders that would employ an environmentally correct approach: the entire home was built from standing dead logs, meaning no live trees were felled for lumber. A craftsman's touch finished the job.

The hard work is evident in every room of the home. Large windows and French doors placed throughout the structure make the log home appear open and airy, while the massive beams afford its refined rusticity. A tree trunk seeming to grow out of the floor adds a touch of whimsy to the living room. And the stone fireplace made of Montana gray rock provides a nice contrast to the orange tones of the surrounding walls and separates the space from the dining room.

Opposite: A traditional stone hearth never felt as appropriate as in this home. **Above:** A sculptural detail in the living room captures the idyllic experience of a log construction.

To adorn the rooms with sophisticated but comfortable furnishings, the owners turned to an interior design team they had worked with on previous projects, though never before on a log home. Their goal was to stay away from log cabin clichés—such as mounted hunting trophies and antlers—in favor of rustic jugs filled with flowers and chunky candles for the mantel. European-style tapestries cover the chairs in the living room, and hand-forged light fixtures brighten spaces, such as the elk silhouettes that hang over the kitchen island.

The kitchen features all the modern amenities one could want, such as a built-in cook top, stainless steel sink, and granite countertops. The bedrooms and baths combine the backwoods style with high-tech features. A whirlpool tub with garden views sits neatly beneath the exposed wood walls and ceilings.

This Page and Left: Sheer craftsmanship achieved such perfectly executed windows.

Left and Above: A private balcony and corner fireplace attend the master bedroom.

The irresistible view of Mt. Sopris is the
backdrop for the Colorado home.

Mountain Retreat

*T*his is not your grandparents' house in the mountains: It's a Colorado retreat, designed with many architectural delights. The house features a modern interpretation of the classic pole barn. First popular in the 1930s during the Depression, the pole construction emphasizes quality and durability over elegance. Here, architect Harry Teague, of Harry Teague used the tried-and-true building technique to create a structure that is at once practical and beautiful. The budget-friendly house is packed with style. Intriguing architectural elements like unexpected angles and artfully placed windows take the exterior from ordinary to extraordinary. Additionally, carefully chosen materials such as sandstone from Eastern Colorado and recycled poplar barn siding found in the Midwest grace the facade.

Inside, exposed beams lend rustic charm, and high ceilings afford an airy atmosphere. The design of the house also takes advantage of the spectacular views of Mt. Sopris. Public areas are located upstairs, where the views are more dramatic. Family and friend can enjoy the large expanses of windows (some of them floor-to-ceiling) in the the living and kitchen areas. The kitchen's open design gives a casual feeling to the space. Homeowners Doug and Linda Hacker can prepare meals while remaining near their guests. Gray-stained pine cabinets with Shaker-like details complement the space, while giving a burst of color to the honey-toned room. Brick covers the floor of the kitchen, and stainless steel further remove the home from the "typical" barn. In an effort to give Linda the restaurant-style look she wanted, Teague incorporated open shelving to keep plates and bowls at the ready. For the counters, the homeowners selected three materials: zinc, soapstone, and stainless steel. Although each is very different, the three materials work well together in the room and give the kitchen a rich layered effect. A dining area and living space are located next to the kitchen. Both spaces are furnished with comfortable pieces that are easy to maintain: a patterned rug and sofa cushions work well because they don't show dirt, while the wood dining table can be simply wiped clean after meals. The easy-going style of the upper level certainly makes guests feel right at home.

Downstairs, three bedrooms and baths provide ample space for the owners and their guests. A mudroom is placed near the entry and connects to the garage. For the floors, another durable choice: poured concrete. Despite its modern feel, the home's architecture and mix of materials boost a rustic aesthetic that is welcoming as it is timeless.

Opposite: The best views in the house are on the second floor. **Left:** Also upstairs, the centrally placed kitchen does not obstruct traffic or sightlines. **Above:** Fishing-lodge style furnishings invite guest to linger.

Grassy green trim and wood shingles relate the
home beautifully to the natural surroundings.

Lakeside
Lifestyle

*R*elaxing, peaceful, rustic—these are the words that come to mind when you first see this Vermont dream home. Set on a gently sloping field fronted by wildflowers, the lodge is designed in the classic Adirondack style. This type of architecture originated in the eponymous mountains of upstate New York during the late 19th Century and is characterized by the use of such natural materials as unfinished lumber and stone. Also called Great Camp style, the original log-construction houses were built for rich urbanites "roughing it" in the mountains. Adirondack houses today are still designed with luxurious layouts, made by local craftsmen, and located on a premium site. Certainly, these same elements are what owners Tish and Dave Richardson had in mind when they found the lakeside site for their vacation retreat—not far from Stowe, a favorite Vermont ski area.

The homeowners turned to local architect Sam Scofield and builder Mike Geoghegan with a specific vision for the house: To create a camp-style structure that also exudes the elegance of European country homes. The rambling exterior with wood shingles and crisp green painted trim complements the natural landscape. The steep roof forms and use of stone are characteristic of the Adirondack style as are the sloped-back chairs that line the porch. Inside, the warmth of the home lives in the abundance of wood details. Beautiful custom-made fir panels, molding, and trim effect that camp-style feeling.

Below: Wildflowers bloom right to the stone porch in the terraced garden. **Opposite:** The focal point of the great room is the two-story Ticonderoga granite fireplace.

Left: Wooded views surround guests in the dining room. **Above:** An undermounted sink and Vermont soapstone counters ease cleanup.

The owners chose fir for the rich honey hue that would have taken pine 10 years to attain. In the great room, the fir panels climb the two-story wall and culminate at the ceiling, which also is lined with wood beams. Elegance and rusticity mix effortlessly in the great room: Leather furnishings, an Oriental rug, Roman shades, and a grand piano give the space a luxurious look, while the double-height Ticonderoga granite fireplace reminds visitors that they are in a ski-lodge setting. From the great room, owners walk through support columns and step up to the dining room. There sits a lengthy 19th-Century oak table flanked by sturdy chairs, wrapped in their original Moroccan leather coverings. A wrought-iron candle chandelier with a leaf motif hangs from the vaulted box-beam ceiling. The pairing of rugged and refined elements attains the camp-style and European sensibilities that the owners desired.

The kitchen takes a more casual approach with wide-plank maple floors and simple cabinetry. The architect took care that the fir of the cabinetry matched the panels—and ordered all the wood at the same time. Even the refrigerator is covered to unify the kitchen's visual theme. For most of the counters and the backsplash, the Richardsons chose Vermont soapstone, a durable and stylish material.

Above: Even the modest vanity receives verdant views. **Right:** A butcher-block island is certainly a country detail. **Opposite:** Half-height windows lend privacy to this downstairs bedroom.

However, the soapstone does need to be oiled regularly to retain its hue and to make it nonabsorbent. Low-maintenance butcher block covers the center island. And tall windows located behind the sink area allow the homeowners to enjoy the wooded views outside, even while doing dishes.

Upstairs, the low roof is intended to give the bedroom a more intimate feeling than the living spaces. Fir paneling adorns the walls of the bedrooms and the baths to promote the warm, cozy atmosphere, and the furnishings and plumbing fixtures have an understated elegance. Throughout, the house is filled with fine materials and crafted with care. In fact, the Richardsons love their second home so much that they've moved in permanently—a true testament to the welcoming architecture and interiors.

The guest suite's balcony wraps around the house, offering a panoramic mountain view. Copper-clad windows will patina gracefully.

Mix
Master

What do you get when you combine French-country accents, Polish pottery, and natural materials such as slate and wood for floors? A handsome mountain retreat with an eclectic look. The owners—Valerie and Gary—are Colorado natives, but lived in Amsterdam for 10 years. Traveling abroad gave these homeowners some new ideas about interior design and a vision of how to display all the furnishings and decorative accessories they had collected during their time in Amsterdam.

In terms of function, the house had to accommodate activities for the family, as well as provide quiet areas for Gary's home office and their live-in nanny. With these goals in mind, architect and friend Karl Krueger created a three-level plan for the structure. Although the home measures a generous 8,000 square feet, the facade is quite modest in scale. A combination of stucco, stone, and cedar bring about architectural interest, and the orientation of the home takes advantage of the mountain views. Practical features like the copper-clad windows that will grow more beautiful with age and a fireproof roof made of Vermont slate let the exterior work as handsomely as it looks.

Continued use of natural materials in the interior creates a smooth visual transition from the exterior. In the living room, for instance, stone and wood bring the outdoors in and meld perfectly with the overstuffed comfortable furnishings. Unique elements in the room include a painting by the architect's mother, a hand-carved wood mantel on the stone fireplace, and plenty of favorite finds from the couple's travels. High ceilings, rich upholstery, and lovely antiques give the space a European ski-lodge feeling. And the choice of durable furnishings, soft fabrics, and low-maintenance materials are comfortable all year round, yet suit the space for entertaining.

The kitchen was the most difficult space to plan, according to Valerie. She wanted a space that was big enough to cater large groups, but at the same time, she desired a cozy setting for the cooking area. Painted in bright hues like cobalt blue, the kitchen's colors were inspired by the homeowners' collection of Italian and Polish pottery. Hickory cabinets, sky blue granite counters, and pendant lighting gives this kitchen its unique, eclectic appearance. The kitchen leads to the dining room through a distinctive opening, where the walls are one-foot thick. The colors in the dining room are more subdued than in the kitchen, and the symmetry in the space offers a very soothing quality.

The master suite, which is located on the main level, also has a calming atmosphere, but with Old World style. Vibrant red curtains frame the spectacular views and a heavily ornamented bed lends European charm. The highlights of the master bath are a fireplace, a steam shower, and the tub that's set beneath wood windows with views of the treetops. Like the master bedroom, the guest suite affords an air of sophistication and comfort, and has a balcony that wraps around the corner of the house. The well-planned layout, use of natural materials, and treasured keepsakes make this house one that is truly enjoyed and appreciated by the homeowners.

Gentle archways define the different activity zones in the main living area.

Overstuffed furnishings balance against the living room's stone surfaces. **Opposite:** A sunny hallway leads from the master bedroom to the dining room.

The master bedroom is compact, but has room enough for
a balcony sitting area. And let's not overlook the view.

Family-Friendly Features

When building a home, you need to consider its occupants and their needs. Here, for example, the home needed to be well-suited for a couple and their young children. Below are some ideas to make your rooms comfortable for the little ones.

- **Easy living**: If you have small children, select durable materials and furnishings. For fabrics, think deep colors and lots of textures to hide dirt. Clearly a white silk sofa is not appropriate with a toddler running around. You may want to consider treating your furnishings and rugs with a stain protector. A caveat: Make sure the stain protection you choose is safe for young children; some contain VOCs (volatile organic compounds).

- **Kitchen smarts**: A simple idea like a breakfast bar is great for teens for their meals on the go. For younger children, consider including lower areas—either a child-size table or a low counter—so kids can have their own space for snacks as well as for doing crafts. Including a spot in the kitchen allows the homeowner to keep young children in their sightline while preparing a meal. Of course, safety is crucial in the kitchen. Be sure to lock up cleaning supplies and place guards on the knobs of the stove. For floors, consider a resilient material, such as vinyl or linoleum, which is softer underfoot and may save your dishes if they get accidentally knocked to the floor.

- **A good layout**: An open plan allows the parents to maintain views of children from room to room. Also, leave plenty of space for kids to roam around. In this house, although there are many fine furnishings and accessories, the architect left ample room between the walls and the sofas for the children to get around.

Nestled into a sloped lot, the rustic home appears smaller than its 5,000 total square feet.

Cabin *Fever*

*L*og houses have appealed to American homeowners since their introduction in the early 1700s, and the structures have not changed much over the last three hundred years. The strong, durable houses possess natural charm and meld beautifully with a mountain setting. Case in point is this house, just outside the Rocky Mountain National Forest in Colorado. Owners Chris and Linda DeMarche had a definite vision for the house: they wanted a traditional log exterior and interior spaces that were modern and unique. They hired architect Alan Carter and builder Greg Glantz to turn their dream weekend house into a reality.

Before the team could begin building the modern log house, they had to overcome some on-site challenges. Local restrictions required the foundation to be built below grade level, which meant blasting almost 7,000 square feet of rock to make room for the house's footprint. Once the site was ready, Glantz brought in "standing dead" spruce logs. The low-moisture logs, which come from trees that are purposely left to dry for several years before they are cut down, are preferred over live lumber for a log construction because they do not shrink and create gaps. Glantz and Carter also salvaged 4,000 square feet of old chestnut planks from a demolished building and used them for the living room floor of the Colorado home. Another rustic touch: The team employed an abundance of stone in the house. In the kitchen, for instance, Wyoming moss rock was stacked to create a stunning two-story fireplace. To create the "contemporary cabin" feeling, the homeowners artfully paired these natural materials with shiny cabinets made with a polymer finish, sleek granite surfaces, and

A large covered walkway outside the front door shelters the entrance from the elements.
Opposite: A 19-foot-tall timber-frame window wall opens the home to its surroundings.

stainless-steel appliances, such as a wine cooler, a professional range, and a commercial refrigerator. Beneath the rugged flagstone that adorns the kitchen floor is a high-efficiency radiant heating system that provides warmth underfoot even on the coldest winter days.

The humble exterior belies other modern conveniences inside. Programmable light controls allow homeowners to set the mood for each room; a high-end security system monitors the property; and the lights, security, and temperature controls all can be operated remotely—even miles away from the house. Finally, the unusual composition of materials used in the central staircase represents the house's duality. Made from hand-cut logs, welded steel rails, and wire cables, the industrial-style stair is a surprise to visitors, while its log details are on theme with the rest of house.

Left to Right: Wyoming moss rock was used throughout the home. Note its variations in color under different light conditions.

Opposite: Wire cabling gives the stairway an industrial edge.
Left: The glass-paneled dining area enjoys views of the Rocky Mountain National Forest. **Above:** The dual-sided fireplace warms the living room and kitchen.

The master suite also combines rugged good looks and 21st-Century design. Walls are made of logs, while elegant furnishings lend a refined quality. The bath has a distinctly modern look with a frameless glass shower and polished-stone sinks with wall-mounted faucets. A soaking tub is surrounded by wood and set beneath windows that offer wonderful views of the Colorado landscape.

The DeMarches also included a luxurious wine cellar, a home theater with a 10-foot screen, a much-needed mudroom, and a guest suite in the house. And when the weather is mild, they can also enjoy a wraparound porch and covered decks. With a comfortable design and modern features, this house lends itself to both family living and entertaining. It is just what the homeowners wanted.

A frameless glass enclosure surrounds the steam shower. **Opposite:** Log walls are 12 inches thick, providing natural insulation against extreme temperatures.

AMERICAN FAVORITES

*D*espite their various influences, the Prairie and Craftsman styles are thought to be indigenous to the United States. The Prairie style, developed by Frank Lloyd Wright, began in the Chicago area in the beginning of the 20th Century. The Craftsman style, founded in California by brothers Charles Sumner Greene and Henry Mather Greene, was popular around the same time. Both styles offer long, clean lines, and low-pitched roofs, and favor natural materials such as stone and wood.

The architects of the homes in this section have revisited these popular styles with an eye toward family comfort. For example, an X-shaped plan creates separate wings to zone different activities, while the wings also serve to give some privacy to the backyard space. A 2,600 square-foot house reminds us that bigger is not necessarily better: An efficient layout and well-planned spaces create an inviting atmosphere. Eco-friendly features make the modest home even more appealing by lowering energy bills. These houses prove that there is a lot of luxury in simple forms and fine craftsmanship.

At one of the rear wings of the house, the family and game rooms provide an attractive entertaining space.

Perfect
Prairie

One of the few architectural genres indigenous to America, the Prairie style was introduced by Frank Lloyd Wright and his group of Chicago architects at the start of the 20th Century. The homes were known for their distinctly planar, horizontal shape that sat low on the landscape. The one-level house shown here, for example, has a unique floor plan designed in the shape of an X. Created by Alan Mascord, the 5,628 square-foot house includes five bedrooms and five-and-a-half baths.

The well-planned layout allows each wing to serve a different purpose. One wing holds the three-car garage, which obviates outside parking in harsh weather. The master suite sits in a second wing, diagonally from the garage. Although it has simple, streamlined design features, a characteristic of Prairie-style homes, the bedroom also includes such luxuries as a see-through fireplace and a flat-screen TV hung from the ceiling, so as not to obscure the beautiful view of the outdoors. The suite's walk-in closet measures an astounding 26 x 9 feet and has two entries, from both the bedroom and the bath. Refined design and modern conveniences mingle in the bath where a double vanity, spa tub, and large open shower offer plenty of room for a couple. A third wing was crafted with a family in mind and holds four bedrooms and a play space, while the fourth houses the family room, game room, porch, and studio.

Throughout the house, honey-toned wood complements the dry-stacked stone used for supportive columns and on fireplaces. Furnishings have a modern look of which Wright

The dining room is entered from the foyer. Just beyond it is the kitchen.

Full-height windows deliver panoramic views of the surrounding property.

Wright On

In 1893, famed architect Frank Lloyd Wright was in his early 20s and started his own firm, after having worked for Louis Sullivan and Dankmar Alder. His first client was William H. Winslow, the publisher of *House Beautiful* magazine. Wright created a residence for Winslow in River Forest, Illinois, that served as inspiration for the Prairie vernacular, and is considered by many the first Prairie House. Made of Roman brick (a brick that is long and skinny), cast stone, and terra cotta, the low, wide structure offered a unique look to the Chicago suburb. The markedly horizontal quality of the house, the overhanging eaves, and the refined amount of detail are all characteristic of the Prairie style. The Winslow House is still standing and is currently privately owned.

would have approved. The lighting design is unobtrusive, mainly incorporating recessed fixtures. In the kitchen, however, pendant lights provide task lighting to the two-level island. A glass counter is set higher than the prep area and is outfitted with tall bar stools. Cabinets feature frameless doors with a streamlined look. Even the hardware is kept simple. Stainless-steel appliances add a reflective quality to the otherwise understated palette. A lively stone floor brings in a bit more color to the kitchen and breakfast area.

The outdoor living space is located neatly in one of the angles of the X design, allowing the wings to lend a degree of privacy. Large square planters, built of stacked stone, are part of the design of the residence, rather than an afterthought. Flowers in vibrant tones brighten the neutral exterior and stone planters. The rectangular pool, also a well-planned feature, not only continues the strong geometry of the house, but also offers homeowners a luxurious spot during the warm months of the year. The angular house, based on one of America's classic styles, affords both stunning style and practicality.

The pitch of the ceiling allows spaces to share light.

A multilevel porch and a pool span the rear, taking advantage of the home's wide footprint. **Opposite:** More intimate spaces are also available.

Energy efficiency starts with a metal roof that
reduces the heat load of the bungalow.

Good
Energy

*W*ith a multiplaned roofline, squared-off columns, and strong geometric forms, this house displays many Craftsman-style features. Yet, the early 20th-Century design is combined with 21st-Century know-how. An all-star team of experts, including architect Sarah Susanka, interior designer Patricia Gaylor, the Bradford Building Corporation, the Building Science Corporation, the Steven Winter Group, and the Florida Solar Energy Center—all U.S. Department of Energy "Building America" members— researched and built the 2,600 square-foot energy-efficient home.

To start, the house has a metal roof, which helps to keep the interiors cool. Plus, self-darkening windows help keep out summer sun, reducing demand on the cooling system. When the darkening feature is not needed, natural light fills the house through strategically placed wall windows and skylights. Additionally, the efficient layout allows the modest-sized house to use less energy than would a bigger house with the same number of rooms. Susanka is known for advocating a philosophy of building better, not bigger. She artfully created this house with a floor plan that includes three bedrooms and a home office on the first floor, away from the noise of the second-floor's public spaces. Varying ceiling heights set the tone for each room. The master bedroom, for instance, has a relatively low ceiling that creates a cozy atmosphere, whereas the tea room showcases a vaulted glass ceiling with blue skies above.

As one tours the rooms, it's obvious that the house is well crafted and beautiful. What is less obvious is the home's environmental sensitivity: Warm-hued natural hardwood and

plush wool carpets cover floors in lieu of man-made products. Synthetic carpets are often manufactured by using hundreds of chemicals, while wool is devoid of such additives. Behind the scenes, the ENERGY STAR®-certified home includes green products like attic ventilation to circulate the air throughout the house and tankless water heaters and heat pumps to heat on an as-needed, energy-efficient basis. Even the furnishings are eco-friendly. Gaylor would not use furniture made from exotic woods. Instead, she chose pieces that were constructed from domestic trees and came from sustainable forests. Natural hemp fabrics adorn the decorative pillows; and many pieces were shipped in recycled paper boxes.

The house, which was built for the 2005 International Builder Show, also includes some luxurious touches that are in keeping with the bungalow style. In the entry, a mahogany door greets visitors, and inlaid borders made of cherry add style to the natural floors. Custom-designed bookcases fill the living and dining

A trim line and accent lighting raises the perceived height of the room.
Opposite: Space-saving built-ins and shelves max out the living room's square footage.

room, providing both storage and display space. In the kitchen, wood, metal, and tile commingle in subdued shades. For the master bedroom, paint in disparate hues, but with the same value, visually expands the space and creates different activity zones. In the bath, recycled glass mosaic tiles decorate the walls while contemporary fixtures, such as a wall-mounted faucet extending from the mirror and a waterfall-like sink, are a surprising break from the Craftsman-style design. Lastly, the house includes a luxurious lap pool outside, fitted with a salt chlorinator that eliminates the odor of chlorine.

The use of green building products, energy-efficient technology, and scaled-down layout fit well with the all-American style. And the careful planning from the whole team of experts will pay off in the long run: The cost of heating and cooling the stunning home is estimated to be $200 a year. Certainly, the new owners—a retired couple—will enjoy both the home's good looks and big savings.

Opposite: The bedroom receives a balanced mix of natural and artificial light.
Left: The peninsula counter is prep area and dining space. **Above:** A vaulted glass ceiling is the crowning touch on the tea room.

Full-height windows and transoms brighten the home's facade.

Craftsman *Spirit*

*C*risp and clean, this 4,776-square-foot house affords charming details and a very livable layout. Inspired by by Craftsman architecture, which began in California and flourished from 1905 to 1930, the exterior includes such typical features of the style as a side-gabled roof, dormers, and decorative stickwork. Often referred to as the ultimate bungalows, the original Craftsman-style houses were generally built on a budget and therefore modest in size. However, they always had a comfortable quality due to an efficient layout. Here, interiors and exteriors have a fresh, uncluttered, desirable ambiance. Designed by Donald A. Gardner Architects, Inc., the facade features many elements—like a series of multipaned windows that line the house and let in plenty of natural light, and a clean-lined carriage-style garage door—that make it appear as if it belongs on an early 20th-Century house.

Walk through the courtyard and columned front porch to an intimate foyer that leads to the great room and the other living spaces. The main floor is segmented into separate areas by the use of architectural dividers. For example, the great room has a massive stone fireplace that not only creates a focal point in the room, but also serves to separate it from the sitting room that doubles as a study. The great room also features a dramatic chandelier made of antlers, rich wood floors, and an exposed-beam ceiling. Wood columns divide the great room from the dining room. From the dining room, friends and family can wander into a wonderful screened porch that is available for use three seasons out of the year. Comfortable, low-maintenance, cushioned seating and a coffee table serves as a spot to relax and enjoy the beautiful views, and another stone hearth provides warmth on colder days.

Above: The three-season screened porch nestles up to a stone fireplace. **Opposite:** Wooden columns and exposed rafters emphasize the great room's refreshing height.

In the kitchen, too, wood dominates—covering the floor, the cabinets, and the refrigerator. A central island gives ample prep space and includes an electric cook-top. A portion of the island curves out and is lined with bar stools for guests to enjoy a snack while the owner prepares the meal. The kitchen measures about 16 x 13 feet, which allows plenty of space to move around and is efficiently designed to make the most of storage and counter space. On one side of the kitchen, the home-owner can wash dishes while looking out onto the side porch of the house. The opposite side of the kitchen includes additional counter space and open shelving to display the homeowner's favorite treasures.

The master suite has its own wing of the house on the main level. Beautiful pic-ture windows topped with graceful curved transoms frame the verdant views. When sited to ensure privacy for the homeowners, windows can be kept bare and sunlight allowed to wash the room. Natural wood floors and an exposed ceiling further blur the line between indoors and out, while neutral-toned furnishings complete the look. Two other bedrooms are also on this floor—each with its own water closet and sink, but with a shared tub. Two more bedrooms, two-and-a-half baths, and a media room can be found on the lower level. Although the design is based on an architec-tural style created over 100 years ago, the house's efficient design and use of natural materials have a fresh appeal and that will definitely stand the test of time.

Opposite: Marble counters offer a crisp counterpoint to natural wood grains. **Left:** Exclusive waterfront views were reserved for the homeowners. **Above:** Updated fixtures in all the home's baths are a whimsical break from theme.

Made for
Relaxation

With four children and busy lives, owners Erin and Jim Moskun yearned for a peaceful vacation home—a place in which to rest and relax, as well as entertain visitors. The homeowners turned to their talented family for help. The design team consisted of Erin's uncle Peter French; her cousin, New York-city interior designer Charles Riley; and her parents—Bette and Byron Riley. The goal, according to French, was to create a house that looked as if it were built in 1905, but also included all of today's modern amenities.

The setting—overlooking a New Hampshire lake—created the perfect backdrop for the getaway. Bette and Byron Riley made sure the landscape had a pristine look with a manicured front lawn and carefully placed potted flowering plants that punctuate the facade with bursts of color. Shingles, stone, and crisp green painted trim commingle to give the exterior a crisp, welcoming appearance. Plenty of open and screened porches allow the Moskuns to enjoy their natural surroundings while protected from the elements. A rounded tower, found on many early-20th-Century homes, not only adds architectural interest to the otherwise linear structure, but also provides a spot to take advantage of the views on three sides. Relaxation is almost inevitable.

From the open layout to the cheerful palette, the interiors continue the appealing, friendly atmosphere. The floor plan was carefully designed to promote an easy-going ambiance. The living room, dining room, and kitchen all flow into one another on the main floor. And the family and their friends can access the wraparound porch through French doors from the

Arts and Crafts-style bookcases flank the stone fireplace. **Opposite:** Recessed into the footprint of the house, the porch is an understated yet integral aspect of the design.

living room—a much-appreciated feature when entertaining. On the main floor, designer Charles Riley selected a mélange of yellows as the predominant color for the rooms. The warm glow of the walls and cooler tones of the furnishings work beautifully with the natural materials in the space. An abundance of wood is used throughout the rooms, such as the cherry and fir floors, the maple chair rail in the living room, and the mahogany kitchen cabinets. To create the look and feel of a 1900s home, many elements in the house are hand-crafted to remind us of the Craftsman-style houses found in the the United States in the beginning of that era. Multipaned windows and traditionally styled furnishings augment the old-fashioned feeling.

The private spaces are relegated to the upper floor of the vacation house. Because the Moskuns have two young children and two teenagers, the design of the bedroom area had to serve different purposes. The master suite, therefore, is situated close to the younger children's bedroom. A space for two little girls, the

Crisp white millwork adds subtle texture
to the rooms. **Opposite:** Other areas in
the home are more cabin-like.

Above: The sauna is large enough for three. **Right:** Plan flooring requires no maintenance and resists fading. **Opposite:** A cushioned window seat makes good use of small spaces.

room is outfitted accordingly with cheerful lavender-and-white bed linens, a cushioned window seat, and hand-painted designs. For the Moskuns' teenagers, French and Charles Riley created a bunkroom that has extra space for friends to sleep over. The teens can also relax in a sitting area that has a high-tech entertainment system. The bath for the kids is kept simple with low-maintenance materials like tile and vinyl floors.

Finally, no stone is left unturned: The basement holds both fun and functional spaces, such as the laundry room, a guest room, a home office, a rec room, and a sauna. The recreation room gives the family a place to get-together to watch their favorite television show, and it also includes exercise equipment. After a good workout, the homeowners or their guests can retreat to the roomy sauna that leads to an outdoor hot tub.

Exposed rafter tails and stone porch supports
are traditional Craftsman elements.

Natural *Blend*

*I*n the early 1900s, two house styles emerged in America: Craftsman and Prairie. Both genres arose from the desire to create homes with simple ornamentation rather than the lavish details common to earlier structures. The Prairie house, first developed by famed architect Frank Lloyd Wright, started in the Chicago area. Wright's first commission—the 1893 Winslow house built in River Forest, Illinois—is often considered the original Prairie house. The design inspired a group of talented Chicago architects to create more houses in this vernacular. The style flourished from 1905 to 1915 and diminished in popularity after World War I. Around the same time, two architects in California, brothers Charles Sumner Greene and Henry Mather Greene, developed the Craftsman style. Influenced by the Arts and Crafts movement in England, the Greene brothers designed what some call the ultimate bungalows.

The historical convergence of the Craftsman and Prairie styles account for the apparent similarities between them: modest scale, low-pitched roofs, and abundant wood details. The home shown here, then, is an anticipated blending of the two architectural styles. Designed by Skycastle Homes, the house's exterior shows many carefully executed details. It has a gabled roof with overhanging eaves and decorative braces—all typical of a Craftsman design—and the multipaned wood door with transoms on top also is characteristic of early-20th-Century houses. The two-story house connects to its garage via a well-crafted breezeway that breaks up the linear quality of the two structures. A combination of square and rectangular windows creates an interesting geometric pattern that is common in Prairie-style homes.

Inside, the designers introduce a touch of contemporary features. The entry foyer, for instance, includes a graceful curved stairway—a departure from the linear forms favored in Craftsman and Prairie houses. The rectilinear layout of the first floor places the formal dining room and living room on the foyer's flanks. Ceiling treatments—coffered in the dining room and vaulted in the living space—lend distinction, while furnishings are kept minimal. The highlight of the family room is a see-through fireplace that separates the conversation area from the breakfast room.

Adjacent to the breakfast area is the kitchen. The open flow of the rooms is ideal for entertaining and affords a sense of ease. The kitchen features beautiful wood cabinetry, a diamond-patterned tile backsplash, and a central island. Stainless steel appliances and a modern stainless range hood add a bit of sparkle to the otherwise organic palette. Two sinks make preparing big meals a snap when there's more than one chef in the kitchen. Delicate pendant light fixtures hang above the island to provide task lighting.

In addition to the living spaces, the laundry room, a mud room, and the master suite are all located on the first floor. Placing the master suite on the first floor allows the homeowners to have privacy from the rest of the bedrooms on the upper floor. The master suite provides a true retreat from the active living spaces. The spa-like bath has a large shower with a bench, a freestanding soaking tub, and gorgeous tile floors with an inlaid design. The suite also includes a sitting area and a walk-in closet. Upstairs, three more bedrooms and two baths offer comfort to family and friends. The contemporary take on the early 20th-Century style home yields a very welcoming design that has a universal appeal.

Just beyond the curved stairway is the kitchen. **Opposite:** A three-sided fireplace unifies the public spaces.

MODERN CLASSICS

$\mathscr{M}$odern" denotes a range of architectural vernaculars, from the International style of the 1920s—with its futuristic forms—to the mid-century modern style, which emerged after World War II. Post-war creativity and technical advances in home construction resulted in startling departures from traditional architecture. Gone were the small, fussy details and flourishes of earlier homes.

This section explores how many professionals and homeowners still feel the great excitement of modern architecture. Whether in a home with a 26-foot-high wall of Mondrian shapes, or a house built in the shape and with the feel of a ship at sea, we see also how beautifully personal the modern home can be. Each chapter features an ingeniously unique, absolutely livable home that fits just right into its neighborhood and environment.

The island's natural landscape
inspired the colors inside the home.

Be Our *Guest*

Set two miles off the coast of historic Southport, North Carolina, Bald Head Island is only accessible by passenger ferry or a private boat. But once there, visitors can roam the island's 14 miles of beautiful beaches and dream of never having to leave. One family realized that dream by building the home featured here. Although the owners planned to use the house as their primary residence, they knew that the serene setting would draw friends and family to visit. So they turned to husband-and-wife architects Chuck and Anna Dietsche to create a functional year-round house that also has the laid-back qualities of a vacation home.

Chuck Dietsche focused on the architecture while Anna worked on the interior design. The couple created a three-wing plan for the home: the first for entertaining, the second for the family's bedrooms, and the third for guests. With the three-wing plan, the shingled house took on a modern layout. In the finished home, traditional features—such as the shingles, a tower, and shutters flanking the windows—sheathe the exterior, but the unique overall shape and elongated forms offer a contemporary flavor.

The same interplay of modern and traditional elements gives a fresh look to the interior. For example, on the walls of the living room, extra-wide bead board (rather than the traditional-width bead board) complements the scale of the space and emphasizes the room's architectural forms. Sleek materials—like glass shelving in the living room and the table in the dining room—and stainless appliances in the kitchen commingle with classic elements like wood floors and trim.

Left and Above: Doors in just about every room access the wraparound deck and, just beyond, the beach.

The chest at the foot of the bed hides a plasma-screen TV.

Throughout the rooms, the refreshing color palette creates a welcoming ambiance. Inspired by Bald Head Island's landscape, the colors include plenty of warm browns and crisp greens. Pale Northern maple lines the floors and is reminiscent of the sandy dunes, and lime-toned furnishings mimic the grasses on the beach. The architects did include some splashes of more intense reds, yellows, and blues. Chuck says that the bright colors signify the saturated tones you might glimpse outdoors, like a passing cardinal.

The owners also possess an eclectic mix of items. They have a collection of contemporary art, a number of Oriental rugs, and some antiques. With that in mind, Chuck and Anna needed to design a backdrop that would balance the disparate items. The predominantly neutral palette with subtle variations in color works well with the homeowners' treasures.

Bead-board siding in different widths add interest to the living room.

Above: The guests' family room includes a kitchenette.

Left: White trim keeps continuity of color between rooms.
Above: "Dimple lights" in the ceiling add sparkle to the dining room.

For the kitchen, the Dietsches created a U-shaped layout. The plan takes advantage of views on two sides of the room—one of the Atlantic, the other of the guest wing. Also in the kitchen are sage cabinets, topped with a pale counter, and a stainless range hood that almost appears sculptural in shape. A casual breakfast area sits beneath two contemporary paintings.

These rooms—along with the bedrooms—were designed with the family foremost in mind. A covered breezeway separates this area from the guest quarters. Housed in their own wing are inviting bedrooms, baths, a living space, a laundry room, and a kitchenette with its own small refrigerator, microwave, sink, and coffee maker. The clever design creates a sense for the fortunate visitor of being in her own beach house—a satisfaction the homeowners feel all year round.

Left and Above: The well-considered floor plan allows water views to take center stage in every room.

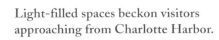
Light-filled spaces beckon visitors
approaching from Charlotte Harbor.

Cracker *Chic*

$\mathcal{S}$et in Boca Grande, Florida—a town with century-old houses—this modern interpretation of a Cracker-style home delights visitors with stylized architecture and a dramatic interior. The Cracker style started in 1840 when early pioneers settled in Florida and Georgia. Since there weren't too many resources for building, houses were made out of locally available materials like cedar and cypress. The structures featured deep porches, so that the overhanging roofs would shield homeowners from the hot southern sun.

To build a 7,500-square-foot home based on such a humble precedent is to embrace simplicity as well as high style. Architects Sam Holladay and Michael Epstein gave the structure a series of clean lines that form almost a neat grid. Porches gracefully line the exterior and give the homeowners and guests covered spaces where they can enjoy the outdoors. Rows upon rows of windows let natural light wash the interiors and set the house aglow at night. The windows also provide a fantastic view of Charlotte Harbor. Named one of the "10 Greatest Places to Sail" by *Sail* magazine, Charlotte Harbor is on the west coast of Florida and features quiet beaches and five National Wildlife Refuges. Of course, the house has all of today's modern conveniences as well, including air conditioning, energy-saving materials, and integrated wiring.

Although the exterior reminds us of days gone by, the interiors are quite contemporary. Under a 26-foot ceiling, the combined living and dining space features a cherry-paneled wall with a geometric design that resembles a Piet Mondrian painting. Openings in the wall

To keep rooms from feeling box-like, windows brighten every corner.

admit light into the staircase behind it. Overhead, clerestory windows set on a diagonal contrast the room's rectilinear wall. The space is finished with ceiling fans, modular furnishings, and open waterfront views. Similarly, the kitchen has a contemporary double-height ceiling with beams that run, again, in a distinct grid pattern. An extra-long island in the center of the space is surrounded by stainless steel appliances and contrasting wood cabinets. A double sink helps homeowners entertain; in fact, the home's large-scale rooms and easy-flowing layout were designed with entertaining in mind—perfect for the sociable owners' cocktail parties and large dinners. Overnight guests retire to the home's two-bedroom guest suite, attended by its own courtyard entrance, living room, and kitchen.

Siebert Architects took precautions to suit the home for a coastal environment. An "island basement" at ground level was designed with walls that can give way to wind and water. "In case of a hurricane, walls would blow out, leaving the concrete-pier foundation and the upper floors intact," says Epstein—a smart feature for a home built just four feet above sea level.

With the charm of the old-fashioned Cracker style exterior, dramatic interiors, smart design, and enticing location, it's not surprising that a design conceived as a vacation residence has become this family's year-round home.

Above: High, lofty ceilings create an airy, open environment appropriate for the coast.

The two-story stairwell is the home's most prominent feature.

Captain's
Quarters

After a fire claimed the original cottage on this Montauk, New York, property, owners Jennifer and Richard Iacono turned to architect Christopher DiSunno (who had designed a neighboring house) to rebuild the home. The house and the property had tremendous sentimental value to Jennifer, whose family had owned the land since 1962. DiSunno's task would be to rebuild the cottage of Jennifer's childhood, as well as draw fresh architectural inspiration from the nearby Atlantic coast and the Montauk Lighthouse.

To that end, DiSunno designed the 4,000 square-foot structure to resemble a ship. The nautical form includes decks that wrap around the house like rigging and a circular "porthole" window. And there's even a spot on the third floor that mimics a captain's lookout, which the homeowners use to watch their children playing below. The interiors feature the fine craftsmanship that you might see on a boat: plenty of wood lines the walls and cabinets and offers a sturdy quality to the rooms.

The entrance greets visitors with the inviting warmth of custom maple panels. Low-maintenance materials like slate and bamboo floors are found throughout the house. The living areas in the house are on the upper level to take advantage of the views, while most of the bedrooms are found on the lower deck—an "upside-down" design. The open plan makes the upper floor conducive to entertaining. Friends and family can easily move from the dining area to the great room. Jennifer loves the space and enjoys having more room than she ever had in the original cottage to host a Thanksgiving meal. Guests also can gather round

Above: Vistawall aluminum frames and custom glass surround the stairwell. **Right and Opposite:** Furniture-grade maple panels with battens add warmth to the interior.

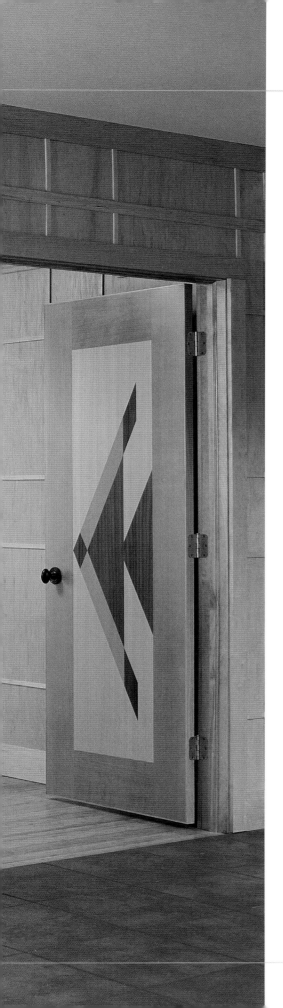

the fireplace on colder days, and in the warm weather the living space expands to the outdoors via the wraparound decks.

The kitchen is both stylish and as efficient as a ship's galley. A combination of open shelving, cabinets, and drawers presents ample storage, while the long countertops provide a good amount of workspace and can serve as a buffet area. Sleek black barstools make room for guests to converse with the cook. And aluminum-framed windows and steel-bar joists provide a cool counterpoint to the warm wood cabinetry.

The open kitchen encourages guests to mingle.

Nautical themes continue to the master bedroom, where custom-shaped circular panes mimic porthole windows. The suite includes a private deck and a luxurious bath—equipped with two sinks, beautiful wood cabinetry, and whirlpool tub. With the great views and modern amenities, the suite gives the owners a place to escape and relax when they're not entertaining or spending time with the rest of the family.

Finally, behind the main structure, the Iaconos included a guesthouse. Set behind the trees, the private suite includes a comfortable living area and one of the architect's favorite features: a stunning pyramid skylight. With so many handsome details and creature comforts, the Iaconos may be just as happy to let this ship stay in port.

Granite countertops match the steel
walkway beams above the kitchen.

Note the bow-like east deck and captain's lookout.
Opposite: Custom windows were made to resemble portholes.

The back of the house shows the existing section from the 1920s and the addition on the right.

Two-Part
Harmony

ts convenient location—less than an hour away from their Manhattan apartment—was what drew the New York couple to this Ridgefield, Connecticut home. The owners knew from the start that they wanted to completely renovate the structure. Originally built in 1920, the house suffered from rambling rooms and poorly designed additions. The homeowners called upon architect Donald Billinkoff to restructure and expand the spaces and interior designer Laura Bohn to create a unique style for the rooms—from scratch.

Rather than attempting to blend the old exterior with the new addition, Billinkoff put the old and new in juxtaposition. A traditional gabled roof tops the existing portion of the house, while a flat roof covers the new section. Similarly, the exterior comprises a contrasting blend of painted-white siding and natural cedar. The unexpected combinations lend the house a contemporary feeling and give onlookers a hint of the modern interior just beyond the front door.

Inside, visitors are received by a large entry hall, which once held the kitchen. The new kitchen is located where the garage had been. In lieu of cars, you'll find plenty of cabinet space, including ones in an L-shaped island with pickled oak, glass doors, and wide drawers; the latest stainless steel appliances, such as two microwave wall ovens and an oversized refrigerator; and low-maintenance solid-surface counters and backsplashes. The kitchen's neutral palette is dotted with color from the beautiful hues of dishes seen through glass doors. And the garage doors have been replaced with French doors, which now lead to the outdoor terrace.

Below: The entry hall makes a statement with its striking artwork and sheer size.
Opposite: A wall of maple paneling conceals stereo and television equipment.

Off of the kitchen is the family room, a stunning space that includes a variety of colorful materials. Maple paneling lines the walls up to the ceiling and and also camouflages the stereo and television equipment. Slate tile covers the floors from the family room to the kitchen and playroom. Streamlined furnishings complete the modern look.

Architecturally, the dining room and formal living room were left intact. Bohn and Billinkoff retained the handsome dark-stained wood floors, but a wall of maple cabinetry in the dining room along with more simple but elegant furnishings maintain the chic ambience found in the new rooms. The master suite remained in the footprint of the original house, but the ceiling has been raised and now includes exposed beams—giving the space a more open and airy feeling than had existed in the room before.

This Page and Opposite: The new kitchen occupies the former three-car garage. French doors with sidelights were fitted into the garage door openings.

Below: A wall of maple cabinetry and streamlined furniture make the dining room quite modern. **Opposite:** Cooler tones inform the master bedroom.

Frosted glass encloses the soaking tub in the master bath. **Opposite:** The enclosed pool features natural cedar siding and a mosaic-tile waterfall.

The highlight of the house is its indoor pool, which the homeowners use as an extension of their entertaining areas (the kitchen, family room, and playroom). Because the home includes the indoor pool, Bohn had to approach the interiors in a very practical way. Rooms needed to be bathing-suit friendly; for instance, the slate floors won't get damaged from watery footprints. And just like the rest of the house, the pool has a modern sensibility—simple cedar siding lines the walls, a huge picture window boasts verdant views, and a waterfall adds even more drama. The stunning renovated home—the new parts and the old—has found new life and completely satisfied owners.

The shed-roof design points the
home toward Sun Valley vistas.

View *Finder*

Picturesque mountain vistas are the backdrop for this Sun Valley, Idaho, vacation house. And architect Jeff Williams made sure to take advantage of the scenic location when he designed the house for homeowners George and Paula Hauer. The Hauers had very specific design ideas; in fact, they sent Williams a video of their former home in Bend, Oregon, showing the architect how they lived and what they liked. They sought a modern house with a rustic flavor.

Given the requirements, Williams developed a unique structure that not only has visual interest, but fits well into the natural surrounding. The roof's shape draws from the Shed vernacular, a type of modern architecture popularized in the 1960s and '70s. A series of exposed roof beams reinforces the home's geometry and branches away gracefully from the structure. The siding has a barn-red hue and oversized windows sited ideally to take in natural light. The result is an exterior that attractively combines old-fashioned styling and modern mechanics.

The reinterpretation of rustic forms found on the outside exists inside as well. For instance, the wood ceiling in the great room features inverted trusses that would feel industrial were the wood not so honey-hued. Central to the great room is a T-shaped fireplace. Here, too, rustic and modern ideals merge with the organic forms of native stone topped by a dramatic horizontal thick wood beam. Windows and doors run from the floor to the ceiling and provide stunning views of Idaho. Furnishings are clean-lined, yet cozy; leather chairs and a generous-sized wood coffee table provide the perfect spot to gather around the fireplace.

The kitchen provides both counter seating and a separate dining space overlooking the terrace. **Opposite:** Inverted trusses create a dynamic living room space.

Oak floors and square framing (which also conceals ductwork) provide continuity of forms from the great room into the kitchen. Once there, you'll see how the Hauers, who are restaurateurs, have planned for serious cooking: Pull-out pantries, high-end appliances, easy-to-clean concrete counters, and devices like heat lamps make this kitchen extraordinary. Additionally, the architect included a built-in knife rack to keep the counters free of clutter. To take advantage of the vistas, glass doors just beyond the dining table lead to the outdoor terrace.

The vacation home is predominantly used as a place for the couple to relax. But in case of a visit from any of the couple's three adult children, the house includes a compact lower level with three bedrooms, baths, and a den. Regardless of surprise visitors, the master suite's placement on the main level, separated from the rest of the home by a hallway, ensures privacy and comfort for the vacationing homeowners at all times.

Credits

10

Mantoloking, N.J.

Design
 John Lederer
 Lederer & Wright
 Partnership
 Bay Head, N.J.
Interiors
 Vicki McLoughlin

20

Winter Park, Fla.

Design
 Rick Thomas
 Intermark Design Group
Builder
 Charles Clayton, III
 Charles Clayton
 Construction
Photographer
 Sam Gray

28

North Carolina

Design
 William E. Poole
 William E. Poole Designs
 Wilmington, N.C.
Photographer
 Jeffery S. Otto
 Hickory Chair Furniture
Plan code
 HPK3000001*

34

Massachusetts

Design
 Mark Schmid
 Dewing & Schmid
 Architects
Builder
 Ed Howland
 Ed Howland Company
Photographer
 Sam Gray

42

New York

Design
 Jerold Axelrod
 Jerold Axelrod &
 Associates
 Commack, N.Y.
Photographer
 Chris Little
Plan code
 HPK3000002*

48

New Jersey

Design
 John Lederer
 Lederer & Wright
 Partnership
 Bay Head, N.J.
Interiors
 Suzette Donleavy
 Well-Designed Interiors
Photographer
 Peter Loppacher

56

Oregon

Design
 Alan Mascord
 Alan Mascord Design
 Associates
 Portland, Ore.
Builder
 Rick Hall
 Richard R. Hall Custom
 Homes
Photographer
 Bob Greenspan
Plan code
 HPK3000003*

68

East Hampton, N.Y.

Design
 Douglas Moyer
Builder
 Ben Krupinski
Photographer
 Mark Samu

78

Florida

Design
 Bill and Greg Weber
 Weber Design Group
 Naples, Fla.
Photographer
 John Sciarrino
Plan code
 HPK3000004*

84

Skidaway Island, Ga.

Design
 Mike Ruddy
Photographer
 Sam Gray

* Construction blueprints for this home are available for purchase.
Call 1-800-521-6797 for details. Refer to plan code listed above.

94

Paradise Valley, Ariz.

Design
Wes Balmer
Builder
Cal Christiansen
Cal Christiansen &
Company
Photographer
Dino Tonn

102

Windermere, Fla.

Design
National Association of
Home Builders
Photographer
Mark Samu

112

Cinncinnati, Ohio

Design
Mike Studer
Studer Residential Designs
Cold Springs, Ky.
Builder
Hensley Custom Building
Group
Ron & Donna Kolb
Plan code
HPK3000005*

118

**Huntington Beach,
Calif.**

Design
David Pacheco
DPA Architecture
Huntington Beach, Calif.
Builder
Stavros Design &
Development
Contracting by Dan Yadgir
Yadgir Construction
Interiors
Margo Hazlett Hazlett
Interior Design
Photographer
Gerry Thomas

124

Florida

Design
Dan F. Sater, II
The Sater Design
Collection
Bonita Springs, Fla.
Photographer
Kim Sargent
Plan code
HPK3000006*

130

Lake Tahoe, Calif.

Design
Sherry Guzzi
Alpine Log Homes
Builder
Alan Richards
A. Richards Built Home
Interiors
Jan Gardner and
Julie Gardner Chesney
Jan Gardner and Associates
Photographer
Sam Gray

140

Carbondale, Colo.

Design
Harry Teague
Harry Teague Architects
Aspen, Colo.
Builder
Mike Conners
Construction
Photographer
Robert Milliman

144

Robinson, Vt.

Design
Sam Scofield
Builder
Mike Geoghegan
The Geoghegan Company
Photographer
Mark Samu

152

Colorado

Design
Karl Krueger
Builder
J. Krueger & Co.
Interiors
The Callicrate Co.
Photographer
Jason McConathy

160

Colorado

Design
Alan Carter
Alan Carter Architects
Builder
Greg Glantz
Raw Hide Construction
Interiors
Kate Bodenhemier
Photographer
Jason McConathy

172

Oregon

Design
Alan Mascord
Alan Mascord Design
Associates
Portland, Ore.
Photographer
Bob Greenspan
Plan code
HPK3000007*

180

North Lake Park, Fla.

Design
Sarah Susanka
Builder
Bradford Building
Corporation
Interiors
Patricia Gaylor
Photographer
Eric Camden

186

South Carolina

Design
Donald Gardner
Donald A. Gardner
Architects
Greenville, S.C.
Photographer
Donald A. Gardner
Architects
Plan code
HPK3000008*

192

New Hampshire

Design
Peter French
Peter French Fine
Woodwork & Design
Company
Norwich, Vt.
Builder
Landscape Design by
Bette and Byron Riley/
The Yardworks
Interiors
Charles Riley
Charles Riley and
Associates
Photographer
Sam Gray

200

Colorado

Design
Scott Rodwin
Skycastle Homes
Boulder, Colo.
Photographer
Tim Murphy
Plan code
HPK3000009*

210

Bald Head Island, N.C.

Design/Interiors
Chuck and Anna Dietsche
Dietsche+Dietsche
Architects PC
Photographer
Gerry Thomas

220

Boca Grande, Fla.

Design
Michael Lee Epstein
Seibert Architcts PA
Sarasota, Fla.
Builder
Peter J. Hayes
Tandem Construction
Interiors
Pamela Holladay
Seibert Architects PA
Photographer
Dan Forer

224

Montauk, N.Y.

Design
Christopher DiSunno
Photographer
Mark Samu

232

Ridgefield, Conn.

Design
Donald Billinkoff
Donald Billinkoff
Architects
Interiors
Laura Bohn
Laura Bohn Design
Associates
Photographer
Mark Samu

242

Sun Valley, Idaho

Design
Jeffrey Williams
Jeffery Charles Williams
Architects PC
Photographer
Roger Wade

* Construction blueprints for this home are available for purchase.
Call 1-800-521-6797 for details. Refer to plan code listed above.